YOUR recipe could appear in our next cookbook!

Share your tried & true family favorites with us instantly at
www.gooseberrypatch.com
If you'd rather jot 'em down by hand, just mail this form to...
Gooseberry Patch • Cookbooks – Call for Recipes
2500 Farmers Dr., #110 • Columbus, OH 43235

If your recipe is selected for a book, you'll receive a FREE copy!

Please share only your original recipes or those that you have made your own over the years.

Recipe Name:

Number of Servings:

Any fond memories about this recipe? Special touches you like to add
or handy shortcuts?

Ingredients (include specific measurements):

D1469231

Instructions (continue on back if needed):

Special Code: **cookbookspage**

Over ➤

Extra space for recipe if needed:

Tell us about yourself...

Your complete contact information is needed so that we can send you your FREE cookbook, if your recipe is published. Phone numbers and email addresses are kept private and will only be used if we have questions about your recipe.

Name:

Address:

City: State: Zip:

Email:

Daytime Phone:

Thank you! Vickie & JoAnn

HOMETOWN
Christmas

Gooseberry Patch
2500 Farmers Dr., #110
Columbus, OH 43235

www.gooseberrypatch.com

1·800·854·6673

Copyright 2013, Gooseberry Patch 978-1-62093-028-1
Second Printing, June, 2013

Check out our cooking videos on YouTube!

Scan this code with your smartphone or tablet...it takes you
right to our YouTube playlist of cooking videos for **Hometown
Christmas**. While there, you can also view our entire
collection of **Gooseberry Patch** cooking videos!

If you spot this icon next to a recipe name, it means we
created a video for it. You'll find it at **www.youtube.com/
gooseberrypatchcom**.

Contents

Dedication

To everyone who still loves a
good snowball fight, building
a jolly snowman and warming
up with a hot cup of wassail.

Appreciation

A most sincere thank you to those
who shared their favorite holiday
recipes and memories with us...
we owe this book to you.

BREAKFAST
with Santa

Mrs. Claus's Gingerbread Pancakes

Jill Ball
Highland, UT

This is our traditional Christmas Eve breakfast. It fits right into our festive mood and gets a fun and busy day off to a delicious start!

1-1/2 c. all-purpose flour	1/2 t. ground ginger
1 t. baking powder	1/4 c. molasses
1/4 t. baking soda	1 egg
1/4 t. salt	1/2 t. vanilla extract
1 t. cinnamon	1-1/2 c. water

In a bowl, whisk together flour, baking powder, baking soda, salt and spices; set aside. In a separate large bowl, beat molasses, egg and vanilla until smooth; whisk in water until well blended. Stir flour mixture into molasses mixture until just combined; a few lumps may remain. Heat a lightly greased griddle over medium-high heat. For each pancake, pour batter onto griddle by 1/4 cupfuls; cook until bubbles form on top and edges are dry. Turn and cook until golden on the other side. Makes 5 pancakes.

Pour pancake batter into holiday-shaped cookie cutters...sure to make little ones giggle! Christmas trees, snowmen and bells are all sweet. Remember to coat the inside of each cutter with non-stick vegetable spray and place a clip clothespin on the side for ease in turning the pancake.

Christmas Waffles

Diane Price
Nappanee, IN

I make these waffles for my family, especially on special occasions like Christmas morning. They are so scrumptious! Make them extra festive by serving with strawberries and fresh whipped cream.

1-3/4 c. all-purpose flour
1 t. baking powder
1/4 t. salt
2 eggs, separated

1-3/4 c. milk
1/2 c. canola oil
Garnish: butter, maple syrup

In a bowl, stir together flour, baking powder and salt. Make a well in the center and set aside. In a separate bowl, lightly beat egg yolks; stir in milk and oil. Add egg yolk mixture all at once to well in flour mixture. Stir just until moistened; batter may be slightly lumpy. In a chilled small glass bowl, beat egg whites with an electric mixer on high speed until stiff peaks form. Gently fold egg whites into batter; do not overmix. Pour batter by 1/4 or 1/2 cupfuls onto a preheated waffle iron. Bake until golden, according to manufacturer's directions. Serve waffles with butter and syrup. Makes about 3 waffles.

Breakfast with Santa is such fun! Ask a family friend to play Santa for the children at your holiday brunch. They'll love sharing secrets with the jolly old elf over waffles and hot cocoa. At the party's end, have Santa hand out little bags of "Reindeer Food"...cereal mixed with colored jimmies for kids to sprinkle on the lawn on Christmas Eve.

Santa's Helper's Breakfast Bake

Ansley Nichols
Marietta, GA

This is a great recipe to put together on Christmas Eve, then bake the next morning while all the gifts are being unwrapped.

1 lb. mild or spicy Italian ground pork breakfast sausage
1 sweet onion, chopped
4 c. frozen shredded hashbrowns, thawed

6 eggs, lightly beaten
2 c. shredded Cheddar cheese
1-1/2 c. cottage cheese
1-1/4 c. shredded Swiss cheese

In a skillet over medium heat, brown sausage and onion; drain. In a large bowl, combine remaining ingredients; add sausage mixture and mix well. Spoon into a greased 13"x9" baking pan; cover and refrigerate overnight. Bake, uncovered, at 350 degrees for 35 to 40 minutes, until a knife inserted in the center comes out clean. Let stand for 10 minutes before cutting. Makes 10 to 12 servings.

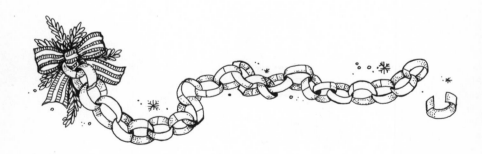

To little ones, it can seem sooo long 'til Santa Claus arrives! Have them make a big chain of paper links and give each link a number from 1 to 25. Every morning at breakfast, they can remove a link...and it's one day closer to Christmas!

Baked Apple Porridge

Nannette Rench
Chesapeake, VA

I like to make this recipe and deliver it to my friends on Christmas Eve as a special gift from my family and me. Top with a scoop of vanilla ice cream for a holiday treat!

4-1/2 c. water
3 c. long-cooking oats, uncooked
2 eggs, lightly beaten
1/2 c. milk or buttermilk
1/2 c. oil
1-1/4 c. brown sugar, packed
2 t. baking powder
1 t. salt
1-1/2 t. cinnamon
2 apples, peeled, cored and diced
1/2 c. raisins
1/2 c. chopped walnuts or pecans
Garnish: maple syrup

In a saucepan over high heat, bring water to a boil; stir in oats. Return to a boil; cook one minute. Remove from heat; cover and let stand for 5 minutes. In a large bowl, combine remaining ingredients except garnish; stir in oats. Spoon into a greased 9"x9" baking pan; cover and refrigerate overnight. Remove from refrigerator 30 minutes before baking. Bake, uncovered, at 350 degrees for 60 to 65 minutes, until a knife inserted near the center comes out clean. Cut into squares; drizzle with maple syrup. Makes 9 servings.

My idea of Christmas, whether old-fashioned
or modern, is very simple: loving others.
Come to think of it, why do we have to wait
for Christmas to do that?

–Bob Hope

Raised Yeast Waffles

Julie Barnes
Bakersfield, CA

We have homemade yeast waffles and raspberry sauce every Christmas morning. This recipe is very easy to double or triple for a big family gathering. Make the batter the night before, refrigerate, then in the morning make your waffles. The sauce can be made with frozen strawberries instead. Delicious!

1/4 c. warm water	1/4 c. butter, softened
1 env. active dry yeast	2 c. all-purpose flour
1-3/4 c. milk	2 T. sugar
3 eggs, beaten	1 t. salt

Heat water until very warm, about 110 to 115 degrees. In a large bowl, dissolve yeast in water. Heat milk just to boiling; add to yeast mixture along with remaining ingredients. Beat until smooth. Cover with a tea towel; let rise in a warm place for 1-1/2 hours. Stir down batter. Cover again and refrigerate overnight, or 8 to 12 hours. Stir down batter again. Pour by 1/4 or 1/2 cupfuls onto a preheated waffle iron. Bake until golden, according to manufacturer's directions. Serve waffles with Raspberry Sauce. Serves 6.

Raspberry Sauce:

2 10-oz. pkgs. frozen sweetened raspberries, thawed and juice reserved	1 t. cornstarch 2 T. light corn syrup

Combine berries with juice, cornstarch and syrup in a saucepan. Bring to a rolling boil over medium-high heat. Boil, stirring constantly, for 2 minutes. Remove from heat; cool, cover and refrigerate. Sauce will thicken as it cools. Serve chilled.

Serve a zingy new fruit drink at breakfast. Mix equal parts chilled pomegranate juice, orange juice and lemon-lime soda or sparkling water. Pour into stemmed glasses over ice...so refreshing!

Crunchy French Toast

Shari Brungart
Sandy Ridge, PA

I make this for breakfast for my 5-year-old son Joshua, and he loves it. He helps me crush up the cereal and pecans...he even came up with the name for it!

6 eggs
2 T. milk
1 t. vanilla extract
1 c. frosted or plain corn flake
   cereal, crushed

1 c. pecans, crushed
1 loaf country-style bread, sliced
2 to 3 T. butter
Garnish: maple syrup
Optional: sliced ripe bananas

In a shallow bowl, whisk together eggs, milk and vanilla; set aside. Combine cereal and pecans in a separate bowl. Dip bread slices into egg mixture; coat with cereal mixture. Melt butter in a large skillet over medium-low heat. Add bread slices and cook until golden on both sides. Serve French toast topped with syrup and sliced bananas, if desired. Serves 6 to 8.

Make fancy bacon curls to garnish breakfast plates. Fry bacon until browned but not crisp, immediately roll up slices and fasten each with a toothpick. Drain on paper towels. Mmm!

Ed's Holiday Bacon Quiche

Gladys Kielar
Perrysburg, OH

Papa Ed makes us our holiday morning breakfast. Using biscuit baking mix for this delicious quiche means there's no fuss over a pastry crust. We hope you'll join our tradition!

3 eggs
1-1/2 c. milk
1/4 c. butter, melted
1/2 c. biscuit baking mix

1/8 t. pepper
8 slices bacon, crisply cooked
   and crumbled
3/4 c. shredded Cheddar cheese

In a blender, combine eggs, milk and butter. Add baking mix and pepper; cover and process for 15 seconds. Pour into a greased 9" pie plate; top with bacon and cheese. Bake at 350 degrees for 30 to 35 minutes, until a knife inserted near the center comes out clean. Let stand for 10 minutes; cut into wedges. Serves 6 to 8.

Fancy-Pants Eggs

Barbara Imler
Noblesville, IN

We enjoy this egg-topped toast at our house for weekend brunch. The toast may be cut into triangles to "fancy-up" for company. Served with fruit, they make a satisfying meal.

1/4 c. butter, divided
1/2 c. onion, finely chopped
1/4 c. cooked ham, finely
   chopped

1 t. dried parsley
1/4 t. soy sauce
4 eggs, separated
4 slices bread, toasted

Melt 2 tablespoons butter in a saucepan over medium heat. Add onion; cook until translucent. Stir in ham, parsley and soy sauce; cook for 2 minutes. Remove from heat. Let cool; stir in egg yolks and set aside. In a bowl, beat egg whites with an electric mixer on high speed until stiff peaks form. Fold egg whites into ham mixture. Spread toast slices with remaining butter; top with ham mixture and smooth out. Arrange toast slices on a greased baking sheet. Bake at 400 degrees for 10 minutes, or until set and lightly golden. Serves 2 to 4.

BREAKFAST
with Santa

Farmstyle Bacon & Egg Gravy

Lisa Kastning
Marysville, WA

This recipe is fresh-from-the-farm delicious and so easy to make!
It's a terrific way to use up some hard-boiled eggs too.

6 slices bacon, diced
5 T. all-purpose flour
1-1/2 c. water
12-oz. can evaporated milk
3 eggs, hard-boiled, peeled and
    sliced or chopped

salt and pepper to taste
Optional: cider vinegar to taste
4 slices bread, toasted

In a skillet over medium heat, cook bacon until crisp. Remove bacon to paper towels and drain, reserving drippings in skillet. Add flour to drippings and whisk until blended. Cook over medium heat until golden, stirring constantly. Gradually add water and evaporated milk; continue stirring. Bring to a boil; cook and stir for 2 minutes, or until thickened. Add bacon, eggs, salt, pepper and a sprinkle of vinegar, if desired. Serve spooned over toast slices. Serves 2 to 4.

Serve up toasty beverages in personalized mugs at your holiday brunch...the mugs are sweet keepsakes guests can take home as a reminder of the day! You'll find a rainbow of ceramic paints and markers at the craft shop.

13

Grandfather's Dutch Bread

Barbara Hightower
Broomfield, CO

Every year my grandmother & grandfather traveled by steam train from Chicago to Denver to spend Christmas with us. Grandfather was a terrific cook, but living in a hotel in Chicago, he had no access to a kitchen. So, when he got to Denver, the first thing he and my mom would do was to go grocery shopping. Among the many foods Grandfather made was Dutch Bread, a delicious cinnamon-sugar coffee cake made from a yeast dough with yummy pockets of custard throughout! I've continued his tradition of Dutch Bread for Christmas morning breakfast, and now, so do my own children and their families. Christmas just wouldn't be Christmas without it!

16-oz. pkg. hot roll mix
1 c. hot water
2 T. butter, softened
3 eggs, divided
1 c. half-and-half

1/8 t. salt
2/3 c. sugar
cinnamon to taste
Garnish: sliced butter

In a large bowl, combine hot roll mix and yeast packet from mix; stir well. Heat water until very warm, about 120 to 130 degrees. Add water, butter and one egg to roll mix. Stir well until a soft dough forms; form into a ball. Knead dough on a floured surface for 5 minutes, or until smooth. Cover dough with a large bowl; let stand for 5 minutes. Divide dough in half. Roll one half into an 8-inch circle; place in a greased 8" round cake pan. Repeat with other half. Cover pans with tea towels. Let stand in a warm place until dough rises a little above the top of the pans, about 30 to 45 minutes. Make indentations, one inch apart, in both pans of dough with a floured thumb. Whisk together remaining eggs, half-and-half and salt; pour mixture evenly into indentations from a measuring cup with a spout. Sprinkle evenly with sugar and cinnamon; dot with butter. Bake at 375 degrees for 15 to 20 minutes, until tops are lightly golden and custard is set. Bread may be baked the night before, refrigerated and warmed in the morning. Makes 2 loaves; each serves 8.

Easy Cinnamon-Pecan Buns

*Sue Klapper
Muskego, WI*

I love to deliver these buns to my friends in disposable aluminum foil pans as a holiday gift. They all love the buttery brown sugar topping of this no-time-to-cook breakfast treat!

1/4 c. butter
3/4 c. brown sugar, packed
1 t. cinnamon
1/4 c. chopped pecans

12-oz. tube refrigerated
Texas-style biscuits,
separated

In a small saucepan over medium heat, cook and stir butter, brown sugar and cinnamon until butter melts. Pour butter mixture into a 9" round cake pan. Sprinkle pecans over butter mixture. Dip one side of each biscuit in mixture; place coated-side up in cake pan. Bake at 400 degrees for 12 to 18 minutes, until buns are lightly golden. Serve warm. Unbaked buns may be covered and refrigerated; give with baking instructions. Best if baked and served within one to 2 days. Makes 10 buns.

Making a list? Check it twice! Use Christmas card clippings to embellish a small notebook...oh-so handy for making shopping lists and schedules. Tie up a stack with ribbon for gift giving.

Deep-Dish Breakfast Pie

Donna Gosdin
Fairburn, GA

This recipe makes two hearty pies...perfect for a brunch or for gift giving! I like to make these pies during the week of Christmas and deliver to family & friends to enjoy over the holidays.

2 9-inch deep-dish pie crusts
2 T. butter, melted
1 lb. ground pork breakfast
  sausage, browned and
  drained

2 c. shredded Cheddar cheese
1 doz. eggs, divided
1/2 c. milk, divided
salt and pepper to taste

Brush the sides and bottom of each pie crust with melted butter. Top crusts evenly with sausage and cheese; set aside. In a blender, combine 6 eggs, 1/4 cup milk, salt and pepper; process until well blended and pour into one pie crust. Repeat with remaining ingredients. Bake at 375 degrees for 30 to 35 minutes, until a knife inserted into the center of each pie comes out clean. If edges of crusts are browning too fast, cover with with strips of aluminum foil. Makes 2 pies; each serves 8.

Baking a homemade pie for a friend? Surprise her by delivering it in a pretty woven pie basket or a ceramic pie plate to keep. She'll love it...two gifts in one!

Christmas Breakfast Casserole

Maureen Wiwad
Alberta, Canada

I have made this recipe for the past few years for our family's Christmas morning breakfast and serve it with fruit salad. It has always been a hit!

6 slices white or whole-wheat
    bread, cubed
1 lb. ground pork breakfast
    sausage, browned and
    drained

1 c. shredded Cheddar cheese
6 eggs
2 c. milk
1 t. dry mustard
1 t. salt

Into a well buttered 11"x7" baking pan, place bread cubes, sausage and cheese. Beat together remaining ingredients in a bowl; pour evenly over bread mixture. Cover with plastic wrap and refrigerate overnight. Uncover; bake at 350 degrees for one hour, or until puffy and golden. Serve warm. Serves 6 to 8.

Santa's Malted Cocoa

Gladys Kielar
Perrysburg, OH

Can you imagine having ice cream for breakfast? At our house, Christmas morning was always special because we knew Papa would serve us Santa's very own cocoa.

2-1/2 c. chocolate ice cream,
    softened
1-1/2 c. milk

6 T. sugar
3 T. malted milk powder
3 T. baking cocoa

Combine all ingredients in a blender. Cover; blend until smooth. Serve immediately. Makes 4 servings.

Tuck silverware into woolly gloves or mittens when setting the breakfast table. Add a knitted scarf to create a whimsical table runner.

Amish Hearty Hotcakes

Patrice Lindsey
Lockport, IL

These are wonderfully hearty, lightly sweetened hotcakes, delicious with a side of bacon or sausage. At Christmas each year, I make this for family & friends as a gift mix packed in bags or jars. I get many requests for the mix throughout the year as well.

1-1/4 c. all-purpose flour
3/4 c. whole-wheat pastry flour
1 c. quick-cooking oats,
　　uncooked
1/4 c. brown sugar, packed
2 t. baking powder
1 t. baking soda
1 t. salt

2 t. cinnamon
2 eggs
2 c. buttermilk
2 T. oil
Optional: 1/4 c. chopped walnuts
Garnish: maple syrup or
　　orange marmalade

In a large bowl, combine flours, oats, brown sugar, baking powder, baking soda, salt and cinnamon. In a separate bowl, whisk together eggs, buttermilk and oil. Stir egg mixture into flour mixture until blended; do not overmix. Stir in walnuts, if desired. Pour batter by 1/3 cupfuls onto a lightly greased hot griddle. Cook until bubbles form on top; turn over and cook until second side is done. Garnish as desired. Makes about one dozen pancakes.

Create a clever gift package for a favorite pancake mix. Fold a bright holiday tea towel in half and sew the two long edges closed to form a bag...slip the mix inside and tie closed with jute. Don't forget to add a recipe card and a big spatula for flipping!

BREAKFAST
with Santa

Pretty Pecan-Cranberry Butter

Paula Marchesi
Lenhartsville, PA

Mom used to make a fancy butter for my brother and me for the holidays when we were growing up. It's wonderful on warm muffins and pancakes. I remember helping her in the kitchen...sometimes I would eat more than I helped, but we always had fun! I've continued the tradition through the years, first with my two boys, and now with my grandchildren.

3/4 c. butter, softened
2 T. brown sugar, packed
2 T. light corn syrup

1 c. fresh cranberries, chopped
2 T. chopped pecans, toasted

In a small bowl, using a whisk or an electric mixer on low speed, beat butter, brown sugar and corn syrup until fluffy, about 5 minutes. Add cranberries and pecans; beat 5 minutes longer, or until butter turns pink. Transfer mixture to a sheet of plastic wrap; shape into a log. Wrap; chill. Makes about 1-1/3 cups.

Honey-Orange Syrup

Brenda Schlosser
Brighton, CO

I love making this syrup in the fall and winter to serve over French toast, pancakes and waffles. At Christmastime, I give it away in pint jars along with recipe cards for my favorite breakfast foods.

3 c. brown sugar, packed
6-oz. can frozen orange juice
   concentrate
1 c. honey

1 lb. butter
2 T. maple flavoring
zest of 2 to 3 oranges

In a large saucepan, cook and stir brown sugar, orange juice concentrate and honey over low heat. In a separate pan, combine butter, maple flavoring and orange zest over low heat. Add butter mixture to brown sugar mixture; stir together. Simmer over very low heat for 5 minutes. Pour into jars; cover and refrigerate up to 2 weeks. To serve, warm desired amount in the microwave for 10 to 15 seconds. Makes 8 cups.

Festive Baked Eggs

Karen Mihok
Valencia, CA

For 25 years, I've made this recipe for Christmas morning. When my children were young, we ate this together after opening our packages as a late brunch to carry us over to dinner. It is now a tradition for three generations.

6 c. shredded Monterey Jack
   cheese, divided
3/4 lb. sliced mushrooms
1/2 c. onion, chopped
1/4 to 3/8 c. red and green
   peppers, thinly sliced
1/4 c. butter
1/2 lb. cooked ham, cut into
   thin strips

8 eggs, lightly beaten
1-3/4 c. milk
1/2 c. all-purpose flour
2 T. fresh chives, basil, thyme
   or oregano, snipped
1 T. fresh parsley, snipped

Sprinkle 3 cups cheese in a lightly greased deep 13"x9" baking pan; set aside. In a large saucepan over medium heat, cook mushrooms, onion and peppers in butter until tender. Drain vegetables well and spoon over cheese. Arrange ham strips over vegetables; sprinkle with remaining cheese. Cover and refrigerate 8 hours to overnight. One hour before serving, beat together eggs, milk and flour in a bowl; stir in herbs. Pour over cheese mixture, using a fork to lightly combine, if necessary. Bake, uncovered, at 350 degrees for 45 minutes, or until eggs are set and cheese is melted. Let stand 10 minutes before serving. Serves 12.

Placecards with whimsy...tie a ribbon around each guest's juice glass, then slip a tiny childhood snapshot under each ribbon!

BREAKFAST
with Santa

Savory Breakfast Frittata

Phyllis Broich-Wessling
Garner, IA

This is one of our winter favorites, sure to satisfy the heartiest appetites! It's especially good on cold mornings, served with slices of fresh tomato and either orange or grapefruit wedges.

4 to 4-1/2 c. frozen shredded
   hashbrowns, thawed
1/2 c. butter, melted
2 c. shredded Cheddar cheese
2 c. shredded mozzarella cheese
16 to 20 mini smoked sausages,
   cut into bite-size pieces

8 to 10 slices bacon, crisply
   cooked and crumbled
8 eggs
1 c. milk
salt and pepper to taste

Place hashbrowns in a lightly buttered 13"x9" baking pan. Spread evenly and press down to form a crust; drizzle with butter. Bake, uncovered, at 425 degrees for 25 minutes; remove from oven. Meanwhile, combine cheeses, sausages and bacon in a bowl; toss to mix. Sprinkle over hashbrown crust. In a separate bowl, beat eggs, milk, salt and pepper; pour evenly over cheese mixture. Reduce oven temperature to 350 degrees. Bake, uncovered, for 30 minutes. Let stand 10 to 15 minutes before serving. Serves 8 to 10.

Celebrate the season with a holiday brunch buffet for friends and neighbors! Make it casual...guests can come when they can and stay as long as they'd like. It's a joyful time of year to renew old acquaintances while sharing scrumptious food together.

Overnight Vanilla French Toast

Kathy Farrell
Rochester, NY

This custardy French toast is a decadent family tradition! Each Christmas Eve, I put together this super-easy recipe before our family fun begins, and pop it in the fridge overnight. On Christmas morning, it goes quickly from the fridge to the oven. When the kids are done opening presents, we all dig into this special breakfast.

1 loaf French bread, cut into
    8 thick slices
6 eggs
2 c. half-and-half
1/2 c. sugar

1/2 t. cinnamon
1/2 t. salt
1-1/2 t. vanilla extract
Garnish: maple syrup,
    powdered sugar

Spray a 13"x9" glass baking pan with non-stick vegetable spray. Arrange bread slices in pan in a single layer; set aside. In a bowl, whisk together remaining ingredients except garnish until completely smooth. Pour evenly over bread slices until covered. Cover and chill overnight, or until most of liquid is absorbed. Bake, uncovered, on center rack of oven at 400 degrees for 35 to 45 minutes, until puffy and golden. Garnish as desired. Serves 4.

Make a scrumptious cinnamon apple topping for pancakes and waffles. Sauté 3 cups sliced apples in a tablespoon of butter over medium-high heat until tender, about 8 minutes. Stir in 1/4 cup maple syrup and sprinkle with 1/2 teaspoon cinnamon. Serve warm.

22

BREAKFAST
with Santa

Christmas Chocolate Pancakes

Kathy Milligan
Mira Loma, CA

We make these scrumptious pancakes on special occasions like holidays with family & friends, birthdays and good old Saturday morning sleep-ins. Yum!

1 c. self-rising flour
1/4 c. sugar
1/4 c. baking cocoa
1 c. whipping cream

1 to 2 eggs, lightly beaten
Garnish: cherry pie filling,
   whipped topping,
   chocolate syrup

In a bowl, combine flour, sugar and cocoa; mix well. Add cream and eggs; stir just until blended. For each pancake, drop batter by 1/3 cupfuls onto a buttered hot griddle or skillet. Cook for 2 to 3 minutes on each side. Serve pancakes topped with a spoonful of pie filling, a large dollop of whipped topping and a drizzle of chocolate syrup. Makes 10 to 12 pancakes.

Get a head start on holiday festivities. Check local newspapers and church bulletins for once-a-year events like craft bazaars, storytelling, caroling and Christmas tree lighting. If you live in the city, check out events in nearby small towns too...such fun!

Star-of-the-East Fruit Bread

Joycean Dreibelbis
Wooster, OH

*Make someone's morning special with a loaf of this delicious bread.
It can be made ahead and frozen, so start now and get a jump
on your holiday baking.*

1/2 c. butter, softened
1 c. sugar
2 eggs
1 t. vanilla extract
2 c. all-purpose flour
1 t. baking soda
1 c. ripe bananas, mashed

1 c. semi-sweet chocolate chips
11-oz. can mandarin oranges,
   drained
1/2 c. maraschino cherries,
   drained and chopped
1/2 c. chopped dates

In a large bowl, beat butter and sugar until fluffy. Add eggs and vanilla;
beat well. In a separate bowl, stir together flour and baking soda. Add
flour mixture to butter mixture alternately with bananas, blending well.
Stir in remaining ingredients. Divide batter evenly between 2 lightly
greased 9"x5" loaf pans. Bake at 350 degrees for 40 to 45 minutes, until
golden. Cool; remove from pans. Drizzle tops of loaves with Chocolate
Drizzle. Store tightly wrapped. Makes 2 loaves.

Chocolate Drizzle:

1/2 c. semi-sweet chocolate chips   2 T. whipping cream

Combine chocolate chips and cream in a small microwave-safe bowl.
Microwave on high for 30 seconds. Stir; microwave an additional
15 seconds, if necessary. Stir until melted and smooth.

Drizzle melted chocolate over baked treats the easy way...dip the
tines of a fork into the chocolate, then do the drizzling.

Helen's Coffee Cake

Robin Horst
Virginia Beach, VA

Grandma Helen always made this coffee cake when we came to visit.
The smell of it baking would permeate the house. I miss her baking
this cake for us, but now I bake it myself. It's so easy and good.

18-1/4 oz. pkg. yellow cake mix
3 eggs, beaten
21-oz. can apple or pineapple
   pie filling

1 c. all-purpose flour
1/2 c. butter
1 c. sugar

In a bowl, combine dry cake mix, eggs and pie filling; mix well. Pour batter into two 9"x5" loaf pans sprayed with non-stick vegetable spray; set aside. In a separate bowl, combine remaining ingredients. Blend with a pastry blender until mixture resembles crumbs. Sprinkle crumb mixture evenly over batter. Bake at 350 degrees for 35 to 40 minutes, until a toothpick comes out clean. Cool; remove from pans. Keep well wrapped. Makes 2 loaves.

Surprise your best friend with a "Tea for Two" party!
Deliver a loaf of Helen's Coffee Cake wrapped up in a tea towel.
Tie on a tea infuser, include several packets of tea...and take
the time to share it with her!

Quebec Maple Bread Pudding

Mitzy LaFrenais
Quebec, Canada

Quebec is one of the largest distributors of maple syrup in the world, so we know lots of delicious ways to enjoy it. This bread pudding is cozy, quick & easy comfort food...it is wonderful for breakfast when you are snowed in!

3 c. white bread or egg bread,
   cubed
Optional: 1/2 c. chopped pecans
   or walnuts
3 c. hot milk

1 c. brown sugar, packed
4 eggs, beaten
1 t. vanilla extract
2 T. butter, sliced
Garnish: maple syrup

Place bread cubes in a greased 9"x9" baking pan. Sprinkle with nuts, if using; set aside. Combine milk and brown sugar in a saucepan over medium-low heat; stir until sugar is dissolved. Remove from heat. Whisk in eggs; stir in vanilla. Pour milk mixture over bread, soaking thoroughly. Dot with butter. Bake at 350 degrees for one hour, or until set. Serve warm, drizzled generously with maple syrup. Serves 4.

Cabin-shaped maple syrup tins make whimsical candleholders for the breakfast table. Tuck tapers into the openings and arrange in a group.

BREAKFAST
with Santa

Sunny Morning Goodness

Amy Hunt
Traphill, NC

This is a country morning, feel-good breakfast everyone will love.

2 T. oil
5 potatoes, cooked and cubed
1/2 c. onion, diced
1/4 c. mushrooms, chopped

1/2 c. cooked ham or bacon,
  chopped
4 eggs
1 c. shredded Cheddar cheese

Heat oil in a large skillet over medium heat; add potatoes, onion, mushrooms and ham or bacon. Cook, stirring occasionally, for 5 minutes, or until potatoes are lightly golden. Add eggs, one at a time, spacing evenly over potato mixture. Cover and cook for 3 to 4 minutes, until egg whites are set and yolks begin to thicken. Sprinkle with cheese; cover and cook over low heat until eggs are set and cheese is melted. Serves 4.

Treat someone to breakfast in bed over the holidays! Fix a pretty tray with a lacy napkin, fresh flowers, the morning paper, a pot of spiced tea and fresh cranberry muffins.

Swedish Tea Ring

Melissa Clemens
Mansfield, OH

I've always loved to bake. When I lived at home, I would make the dough the night before, then pop it in the oven on Christmas morning. After we opened our presents, we would enjoy a slice with our coffee...delicious!

2 1-lb. loaves frozen bread
   dough, thawed
2 T. butter, softened
1/2 c. brown sugar, packed

2 t. cinnamon
Garnish: chopped nuts,
   candied cherries

On a lightly floured surface, combine both loaves of dough. Roll out together into a 15-inch by 7-inch rectangle. Spread with butter. In a small bowl, mix brown sugar and cinnamon; sprinkle over butter. Roll up dough tightly, beginning at one long edge. Seal lengthwise by pinching together. Place seam-side down on a lightly greased baking sheet; pinch ends together to form a ring. With kitchen scissors, cut 2/3 way through the ring at one-inch intervals. Turn each section on its side. Let rise until double, 35 to 40 minutes. Bake at 375 degrees for 25 to 30 minutes. While still warm, drizzle with Powdered Sugar Icing; decorate with nuts and cherries. Serve warm. Makes 12 servings.

Powdered Sugar Icing:

1 c. powdered sugar
1-1/2 T. whipping cream

1/2 t. vanilla extract

Mix together all ingredients to a drizzling consistency.

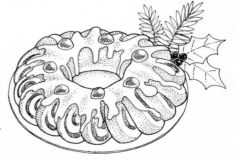

A friend who bakes would love to find a cookbook slipped in the pocket of a potholder. Don't forget to tuck in recipe cards sharing some family favorites too.

Peach Coffee Cake

Lanita Anderson
Chesapeake, VA

A friend in my Bible study group brought this coffee cake one day for our fellowship time...it was so scrumptious, we all asked for the recipe! It's a great Christmas Eve light dessert to share and makes a wonderful Christmas morning brunch treat too.

18-1/4 oz. pkg. yellow cake mix
3 eggs, beaten
1 t. lemon extract, divided
21-oz. can peach pie filling, cut
   into smaller pieces

1/2 c. chopped walnuts
1/2 c. sugar
1/2 c. all-purpose flour
1/4 c. butter, softened

In a large bowl, combine dry cake mix, eggs, 1/2 teaspoon extract, pie filling and walnuts. Stir until well blended. Spread batter in a greased and floured 13"x9" baking pan; set aside. In a separate bowl, mix sugar, flour, butter and remaining extract with a fork or pastry blender until crumbly. Sprinkle evenly over batter. Bake at 350 degrees for 40 to 45 minutes, until center of cake springs back when touched. Makes 12 servings.

Warm breakfast casseroles and freshly baked coffee cakes travel well in insulated containers...perfect for a snowy picnic after cutting down the Christmas tree. Add a thermos of hot cocoa. Memories in the making!

Maple-Pecan Muffins

Tina George
El Dorado, AR

A family favorite with hot cocoa or coffee on a cold morning! The kids always came running when the scent of these muffins filled the air. Now that they're grown, I make these muffins on Christmas morning when we all gather for breakfast.

2 c. all-purpose flour
1/4 c. light brown sugar, packed
1-1/2 t. baking powder
1/4 t. salt
1 egg
1/2 c. milk

1/2 c. maple syrup
1/3 c. margarine, melted
1 t. vanilla extract
1 c. chopped pecans
1 T. sugar
1/8 t. cinnamon

In a large bowl, mix flour, brown sugar, baking powder and salt. In a small bowl, beat egg, milk, syrup, margarine and vanilla. Add egg mixture to flour mixture; stir just until moistened. Batter will be lumpy. Stir in pecans. Spoon batter into paper-lined or greased muffin cups, filling 2/3 full. Mix sugar and cinnamon in a cup; sprinkle over batter. Bake at 400 degrees for 15 to 20 minutes, until golden and a toothpick tests clean. Serve warm. Makes one dozen.

Tuck a packet of Maple-Pecan Muffins into a pretty gift basket of breakfast foods like flavored coffees, jams & jellies...a thoughtful gift that's sure to be appreciated.

BREAKFAST
with Santa

Aunt Pearl's Breakfast Scones
Pearl Teiserskas
Brookfield, IL

This recipe was given to me back in the 1950s by a very dear friend. It is simple yet oh-so good, especially with homemade jam or jelly. You can improvise and add any ingredients you prefer. Make them your own with dried cranberries or blueberries or chopped nuts.

1-3/4 c. all-purpose flour
5 T. sugar
2-1/2 t. baking powder
1/2 t. salt
1/3 c. butter

1/2 c. currants, raisins or
   dried cherries
2 eggs, divided
4 to 6 T. half-and-half

In a large bowl, combine flour, sugar, baking powder and salt. Cut in butter until mixture resembles fine crumbs. Stir in fruit, one beaten egg and just enough half-and-half for dough to leave the sides of the bowl. Turn dough onto a lightly floured surface; knead lightly. Roll out dough 1/2-inch thick; cut out with a floured 2-1/4" biscuit cutter. Place scones on an ungreased baking sheet; brush with remaining beaten egg. Let stand for 5 to 10 minutes. Bake at 400 degrees for 10 to 12 minutes, until golden. Immediately remove from baking sheet. Makes 8 scones.

Bela's Famous Hot Cocoa
Julie Dossantos
Fort Pierce, FL

My daughter Isabela and I created this delicious hot cocoa recipe to give as Christmas gifts one year. Enjoy!

2 c. powdered milk
1/2 c. powdered non-dairy
   creamer
1 c. sugar

1/2 c. baking cocoa
1 t. cinnamon
1 dash salt

Mix together all ingredients in a large bowl. Keep in a covered container or place in jars or bags for gift giving, with directions attached. To use: Add 3 to 4 generous tablespoonfuls of cocoa mix to a mug. Add 3/4 to one cup boiling water (depending on size of mug) and stir well. Makes 10 to 12 servings.

Hungarian Coffee Cake

Kristin Price
Croton, OH

For over 40 years, this delicious coffee cake has been our Christmas morning favorite. For the best flavor, use real butter and full-fat sour cream.

2 c. all-purpose flour
1 c. sugar
1 c. brown sugar, packed
1 c. butter
2 eggs, beaten

1 c. sour cream
1-1/4 t. baking soda
3/4 t. salt
1 t. vanilla extract
1/4 c. chopped walnuts or pecans

Combine flour, sugars and butter in a large bowl; mix with a fork until crumbly. Reserve one cup of mixture for topping. Add eggs, sour cream, baking soda, salt and vanilla to flour mixture; stir lightly. Pour batter into 2 lightly greased 9" round cake pans. Sprinkle evenly with reserved flour mixture and nuts. Bake at 350 degrees for about 30 minutes. Let cool for 15 minutes; drizzle with red and green icing in a criss-cross pattern. Makes two coffee cakes; each serves 8.

Red & Green Icing:

1 c. powdered sugar
1/2 t. orange extract
1 T. water

small amount red and green
paste food coloring

Stir together powdered sugar, extract and enough water to make a drizzling consistency. Divide into two smaller bowls; tint each with food coloring.

Years ago, Christmas gifts were much simpler. Recall those times with charming table favors. Fill brown paper lunch sacks with a juicy orange, a popcorn ball, some nuts and some old-fashioned hard candies. Tie with yarn and set one at each place. So sweet!

BREAKFAST
with Santa

Christmas Sausage & Swiss Bake

Tammy Dalton
Jeromesville, OH

My mom always fixed this simple dish for Christmas morning to serve with fresh fruit salad and blueberry muffins. Yummy!

10 eggs
1 c. evaporated milk
4 slices bread, cubed
1/2 t. dry mustard

2 c. shredded Swiss cheese
1 lb. ground pork breakfast
   sausage, browned and
   drained

In a large bowl, beat together eggs and milk. Stir in remaining ingredients. Spoon into a 13"x9" baking pan sprayed with non-stick vegetable spray. Cover and refrigerate 4 hours to overnight. Bake, uncovered, at 350 degrees for 40 to 45 minutes, until eggs are set in the center and top is golden. Serves 6 to 9.

Tasty Fruit Salad

Marian Bates
Stephen, MN

I got this recipe from the pastor's wife at our Presbyterian church. It's terrific in winter...I've used it often in the past 20 years. If you like, add a can of mandarin oranges and a few maraschino cherries for some festive color.

20-oz. can pineapple chunks in
   juice, drained and 3/4 c. juice
   reserved
2 apples, cored and cubed
2 bananas, sliced

1/2 c. sugar
2 T. cornstarch
1 t. orange zest
1 T. orange juice
1 T. lemon juice

Combine fruit in a bowl; set aside. Add reserved pineapple juice and remaining ingredients to a saucepan. Heat to boiling over medium-high heat. Boil one minute, stirring constantly. Pour hot dressing over fruit mixture; toss to coat. Cover and chill. Serves 8.

Tie tiny Christmas ornaments onto stemmed glasses with ribbon bows...so festive for serving orange juice at a holiday brunch.

Cinnamon-Apple Compote

Lisa McClelland
Columbus, OH

In my family, this is a favorite topping for oatmeal waffles.
It's even good with roast pork...enjoy!

2 T. butter
3 Pink Lady or Granny Smith
   apples, peeled, cored and
   cubed
3 Gala or Fuji apples, peeled,
   cored and thinly sliced
2 t. lemon juice

2 t. cinnamon
1/8 t. sea salt
1 c. water, divided
1/3 c. honey
1 t. vanilla extract
Optional: 1 T. apple brandy

In a large saucepan, melt butter over medium heat until bubbly. Add cubed apples; sauté for about 5 minutes, until they begin to release their juice. Add sliced apples; toss to coat well. Sprinkle with lemon juice, cinnamon, salt and a small amount of water, if mixture is dry. Increase heat to high and bring to a boil; add a little more water to keep apples from sticking. Reduce heat to low. Cover and cook for about 30 minutes, stirring often and adding more water as necessary. When cubed apples are fork-tender but still well formed and sliced apples are very soft, add remaining ingredients. Stir; cook for one minute. Increase heat; simmer for one more minute; stir. Adjust seasonings to taste, adding more honey, vanilla or cinnamon, as desired. Serve warm. Makes 2 cups.

Snow globes are a quick craft to make with children. Use silicone glue to secure a mini plastic or ceramic figure to the inside of a jar lid; let dry. Fill the jar almost to the top with distilled water, a pinch of glitter and a dash of glycerin to keep the glitter from falling too quickly. Tighten the lid and let it snow!

SLEDDING
Party Warmers

Snow-Day Vegetable Chowder

Bethi Hendrickson
Danville, PA

Serve up homemade vegetable soup and fresh-baked cornbread for warm tummies on cold winter days!

5 carrots, peeled and diced
2 onions, chopped
2 T. butter
4 c. chicken broth
2 potatoes, peeled and diced
6 c. corn

2 c. fat-free half-and-half
3 T. cold water
3 T. cornstarch
1-1/2 t. salt
Garnish: chopped fresh parsley

In a large stockpot, sauté carrots and onions in butter. Add broth; bring to a boil. Add potatoes and corn; stir in half-and-half. Reduce heat to medium. Simmer 15 minutes, until vegetables are tender. In a small bowl, mix cold water and cornstarch until smooth. Thin with a small amount of soup broth; stir into soup. Add salt. Simmer 5 minutes, until thickened. Garnish with parsley. Serve with Miss Marlene's Cornbread. Makes 8 servings.

Miss Marlene's Cornbread:

1-1/2 c. cornmeal
1/2 c. all-purpose flour
2 t. baking powder
1 T. sugar
1 t. salt

1/2 t. baking soda
1/4 c. shortening or bacon
    drippings
1-1/2 c. buttermilk
2 eggs, beaten

Combine all ingredients in a bowl; beat vigorously for 30 seconds. Pour into a greased 8"x8" baking pan or a cast-iron skillet. Bake at 450 degrees until golden, 25 to 30 minutes. Serve warm. Serves 8.

Crunchy bread sticks are tasty soup dippers! Stand them up in a tall, wide flower vase...they'll take up little space on a soup buffet.

SLEDDING
Party Warmers

Hearty Hamburger Veggie Soup

Lori Ritchey
Narvon, PA

Every Christmas, our church presents a Living Nativity scene. Several ladies and gentlemen of our congregation bring crocks of soup to keep the actors warm when they are a part of the scenes outside. Everyone enjoys the food & fellowship in the church kitchen...this soup has become a favorite! The recipe can easily be doubled to feed more.

1 lb. lean ground beef
1 T. garlic powder
14-1/2 oz. can Italian-seasoned
   diced tomatoes
2 10-1/2 oz. cans beef broth

16-oz. pkg. frozen soup
   vegetables
1 T. onion powder
1 t. pepper
1 T. Worcestershire sauce

In a large stockpot over medium heat, brown beef with garlic powder; drain. Add tomatoes with juice and remaining ingredients; bring to a boil. Reduce heat to low; simmer for about 45 minutes, stirring occasionally. Serves 6 to 8.

Making a favorite soup for supper? Let the slow cooker help out! In the morning, toss in all the ingredients and turn it to the low setting. A recipe that simmers for one to two hours on the stovetop can usually cook all day on low without overcooking.

Chicken Noodle Soup

Glorya Hendrickson
Hesperia, CA

My family loves this soup year 'round, but especially on cold, rainy days! If you like a chicken noodle soup with more broth, add fewer noodles, as they will absorb the broth as the soup stands.

1 c. onion, chopped
1 c. celery, chopped
1/4 c. butter
1 c. carrots, peeled and chopped
12 c. water
3 T. chicken bouillon granules

4 c. cooked chicken, chopped
1/2 t. dried marjoram
1/4 t. pepper
1 bay leaf
2 c. thin egg noodles, uncooked
1 T. fresh parsley, chopped

Cook onion and celery in butter in a large Dutch oven until tender. Add remaining ingredients except noodles and parsley; bring to a boil. Reduce heat to low; cover and simmer for 30 minutes. Remove bay leaf; stir in noodles and parsley. Cook over medium heat for 10 minutes, stirring occasionally, or until noodles are tender. Makes 8 servings.

Cheer up a friend who's home with the sniffles. Fill a fabric-lined basket with a big jar of Chicken Noodle Soup, some oyster crackers, a soup mug and a cheerful book to read while recovering.

Creamy Broccoli Soup

Tammie Douglas
Ossian, IN

This is such a quick & easy recipe for a cozy night at home...
perfect after a day of Christmas shopping.

2 10-3/4 oz. cans cream of
    mushroom soup
1-1/2 c. milk
8-oz. pkg. cream cheese, cubed

1/2 c. onion, finely chopped
12-oz. pkg. frozen chopped
    broccoli, thawed
garlic salt to taste

Place all ingredients in a heavy saucepan. Cook over medium heat until broccoli is tender and cream cheese is melted, 10 to 15 minutes. Makes 4 to 6 servings.

For a festive garnish on bowls of hot soup,
use a mini cookie cutter to cut star shapes from
slices of bread.

Ham & Turnip Greens Soup

Lindy Acree
Fairbanks, LA

*Whenever my mother made this soup, I would not try it because
I hated turnip greens. One day she insisted that I try it "just one time,"
and now I am hooked. Thanks to Mom, now I know what I was
missing all that time!*

1 c. potatoes, peeled and chopped	4 14-1/2 oz. cans chicken broth
1 c. onion, chopped	16-oz. pkg. frozen turnip greens
1 c. carrots, peeled and sliced	2 16-oz. cans Great Northern
1 c. celery, chopped	beans, drained and rinsed
3 T. olive oil	2 c. cooked ham, diced

In a large stockpot over medium heat, sauté potatoes, onion, carrots and
celery in olive oil for about 15 minutes, until tender. Add remaining
ingredients; reduce heat to medium-low. Cover and cook for 45 minutes,
stirring occasionally. Makes 12 to 15 servings.

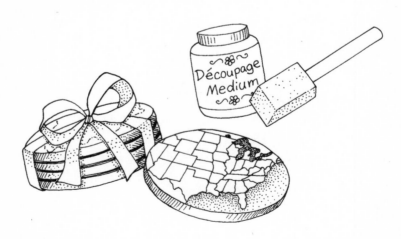

Whip up a stack of map coasters...a useful souvenir of hometown
or vacation memories! Trace around cork coasters onto paper
maps and cut out. Brush backs of cut-outs with découpage
medium and press onto coasters. Smooth out any bubbles.
When dry, brush the fronts with another layer or two
to protect the coasters.

SLEDDING
Party Warmers

Mom's Corn Chowder

Melissa Knight
Athens, AL

When I was in the third grade, my family and I lived in Louisville, Kentucky. One January morning, we awoke to find over 15 inches of unexpected snow on the ground! I still remember Mom making this delicious chowder with ingredients she had on hand...so cozy!

4 potatoes, peeled and cubed
1/8 t. salt
2 onions, diced
1/4 c. butter

2 14-3/4 oz. cans creamed corn
4 c. milk
5-oz. can evaporated milk
1/8 t. pepper

Cover potatoes with water in a large Dutch oven; add salt. Bring to a boil over medium-high heat; cook until nearly tender. Meanwhile, in a separate saucepan over medium heat, sauté onions in butter until tender. Add onion mixture to cooked potatoes; do not drain potatoes. Stir in remaining ingredients. Simmer over low heat for at least 30 minutes, stirring occasionally. Serves 4 to 6.

Fizzle Biscuits

Brenda Hughes
Houston, TX

I can't forget my husband's face after taking his first bite of these biscuits...he loved them! Homemade made easy.

1/4 c. butter, melted
1/2 c. sour cream

2 c. biscuit baking mix
1/2 c. lemon-lime soda

Spread melted butter in a 8"x8" baking pan; set aside. In a bowl, cut sour cream into biscuit mix with a pastry cutter. Add soda; stir until a very soft dough forms. Drop dough evenly by large spoonfuls over butter, making 9 biscuits. Bake at 450 degrees for 10 to 12 minutes, until golden. Makes 9 biscuits.

Share the holiday spirit with a good winter deed! Shovel the driveway and sidewalk for a neighbor.

Meatless Borscht

Louise Maksymetz
Manitoba, Canada

This is my grandmother's recipe. It is a family tradition to serve this meatless soup for Christmas Eve supper.

3 beets, peeled and diced
1 carrot, peeled and diced
8 c. water
1 potato, peeled and diced
2 T. lemon juice
1/2 c. green beans
1/2 c. peas
1 onion, sliced

3 T. butter
1-1/2 c. cabbage, shredded
1/4 c. warm water
1 c. tomato juice, or 10-3/4 oz.
    can tomato soup
1/2 c. cold water
1-1/2 T. all-purpose flour
Garnish: chopped fresh dill

In a large stockpot, combine beets, carrot and water. Simmer over medium heat for 20 minutes. Add potato; simmer for 10 to 15 minutes. Stir in lemon juice, beans and peas; simmer until tender. Meanwhile, in a separate saucepan over medium heat, sauté onion in butter until soft. Add cabbage and warm water to onion; simmer until cabbage is tender. Add cabbage mixture and tomato juice or soup to beet mixture. Blend cold water and flour; stir into soup. Bring to a boil; cook and stir just until thickened. Sprinkle portions with dill. Serves 12 to 15.

Make an Advent wreath to count the weeks to Christmas. Lay an evergreen wreath flat and space four candles around it. Each Sunday before Christmas, your family can light an additional candle.

SLEDDING
Party Warmers

Mom's Kielbasa Stew

Holli Purkeypile
Holyoke, CO

Years ago, my mom and I were putting together a family cookbook. Sadly, she passed away and we never finished it. When my family moved, I found the unfinished project in a dust-covered box under the bed. I finished the cookbook and had it printed in her memory. I am so glad that I did, because I have found some of the best "forgotten" recipes in it, including this one!

1 lb. Polish sausage, sliced
    1/2-inch thick
3 c. chicken broth, divided
1 c. onion, chopped

1 T. garlic, minced
2 16-oz. cans navy beans
1/2 lb. cabbage, chopped

In a stockpot over medium heat, brown sausage. Drain; remove sausage and set aside. To the same pot, add one cup broth, onion and garlic. Bring to a boil over high heat; simmer until onion is tender. Stir in remaining broth, beans and cabbage; return sausage to pan. Reduce heat to medium-low; cover and simmer for 20 to 30 minutes, until cabbage is tender. Makes 6 servings.

Invite friends over for a soup supper on a frosty winter evening. Ask everyone to bring their favorite soup or bread to share, as well as good company! You provide the bowls, spoons, cookies for dessert and a crackling fire.

Hearty Pizza Soup ▶️

Renae Scheiderer
Beallsville, OH

*I make this savory soup during the cold winter months...
it's requested often!*

1 lb. ground Italian pork sausage
1/2 c. onion, chopped
1/2 c. green pepper, chopped
4-1/4 c. water, divided
1/2 t. Italian seasoning
1/4 t. garlic powder
1/4 t. dried basil
1/8 t. dried rosemary

1/8 t. salt
1/8 t. pepper
2 15-oz. jars pizza sauce
2 tomatoes, chopped
6-oz. pkg. pepperoni, chopped
Garnish: shredded mozzarella
    cheese, chopped mushrooms

Brown sausage in a skillet over medium heat; drain. Add onion, green pepper and 1/4 cup water; sauté until tender. Stir in seasonings. In a large saucepan over medium heat, combine pizza sauce, remaining water, tomatoes, pepperoni and sausage mixture. Bring to a boil; reduce heat to medium-low and simmer for about 15 minutes. At serving time, top each bowl with shredded cheese and chopped mushrooms. Makes 4 to 6 servings.

Old-fashioned Christmas bazaars are so much fun...jot down the dates on your calendar and invite girlfriends to come along. These get-togethers are filled with one-of-a-kind handmade items and scrumptious homebaked goodies that are just too good to pass up!

Christmas Hot Broth

Barbara Imler
Noblesville, IN

One Christmas many years ago, I received a jar of this broth along with the recipe from a dear neighbor who has since passed on. It's so good on cold winter days...I love to make it during the holidays.

4 c. cocktail vegetable juice
2 c. chicken broth
1/4 c. sherry or chicken broth

2 T. brown sugar, packed
1 T. butter, melted

Combine all ingredients in a large saucepan. Heat over medium-low heat; do not allow to boil. Serve in mugs. Makes 6 servings.

Spicy Pantry Soup

Laura Lane
Carthage, MO

This is a terrific emergency dinner...I like to keep these ingredients on hand in the pantry, just in case!

15-1/2 oz. can black beans
11-oz. can sweet corn & diced
  peppers
10-oz. can diced tomatoes with
  green chiles

1-1/4 oz. pkg. taco seasoning
  mix
Garnish: shredded cheese,
  crushed tortilla chips

Mix all ingredients except garnish in a saucepan over medium heat. Simmer, stirring occasionally, for 5 to 10 minutes. Garnish as desired. Makes 4 to 6 servings.

String popcorn and cranberries together for some old-fashioned family fun. The kids will love it, and the strands are so pretty draped along a mantel, a doorway and on the Christmas tree.

Baked Fish Chowder

Peg Hebden
Melvin Village, NH

Hearty, comforting and oh-so easy to make!

2 lbs. cod or haddock fillets
4 potatoes, peeled and diced
3 onions, sliced
1 clove garlic, pressed
1/2 c. celery leaves, chopped
4 whole cloves
1 bay leaf

1/4 t. dill weed
salt to taste
2 c. boiling water
Optional: 1/4 c. dry vermouth
2 c. light cream
Garnish: oyster crackers

Combine all ingredients except cream and garnish in a 4-quart casserole dish; stir. Cover and bake at 375 degrees for one hour. Shortly before serving time, discard cloves and bay leaf. In a saucepan over medium-low heat, warm cream just to boiling. Stir cream into chowder, gently breaking up fish fillets. Serve topped with crackers. Makes 6 to 8 servings.

At Christmas, when old friends are meeting,
We give that long-loved joyous greeting:
Merry Christmas!

–Dorothy Brown Thompson

Mom's Special Oyster Stew

Jennifer Babcock
North Collins, NY

Christmas Eve is my favorite day! My family always starts by opening the stockings that Santa has left as a preview of what is to come. Then we begin our feast! Appetizers like shrimp cocktail, cheese & crackers, and always my mom's oyster stew, which she insists brings good luck throughout the year. With just four ingredients, real butter and whole milk really make a difference in the oyster stew. Our main course is more seafood. It's just such a magical time...I look forward to it every year!

1 pt. fresh oysters
1/2 c. butter

2 c. whole milk
salt and pepper to taste

Pour oysters with their broth into a saucepan; add butter. Cook over low heat until butter is melted and oysters' edges curl. Add milk, salt and pepper. Gently heat through without boiling. Makes 8 servings.

Kids just can't wait 'til Christmas? Celebrate early on
Saint Nicholas Day, December 6th! Each child sets out his or
her shoes the night before...Saint Nick will fill the shoes
of those who've behaved with treats and small gifts.

Diane's Turkey Chili

Diane Widmer
Blue Island, IL

I created this mild-tasting recipe for my friends who love chili, but can't eat red meat or very spicy food. They all like it!

1 lb. lean ground turkey
1/2 c. onion, chopped
1 t. garlic, minced
1 t. dried oregano
1 t. chili powder
14-1/2 oz. can petite diced
    tomatoes

1/2 c. spaghetti sauce
3/4 c. tomato soup
15-1/2 oz. can kidney beans,
    drained and rinsed
Garnish: shredded Cheddar
    cheese, oyster crackers

In a skillet over medium heat, brown turkey with onion and garlic. Drain; sprinkle with seasonings. Stir; add remaining ingredients except garnish. Reduce heat to medium-low. Cover; simmer for 20 to 25 minutes, until heated through. Serve topped with cheese and crackers. Makes 4 servings.

Give a gift card, plus a little extra! Cut a card-sized pocket
from felt. Stitch or hot glue it to the front of a Christmas
stocking to form a pocket for the gift card. Slip a little
homemade gift into the stocking to go with the card.

Pepper Jack Corn Muffins

Vickie

A basket of these warm muffins is wonderful alongside your favorite chili or taco soup.

1-1/2 c. yellow cornmeal
1 t. salt
1/4 t. baking soda
2 eggs, beaten
3/4 c. sour cream

1/4 c. oil
14-3/4 oz. can creamed corn
3/4 c. shredded Pepper Jack
   cheese, divided

In a large bowl, combine cornmeal, salt and baking soda; set aside. In a small bowl, whisk together eggs, sour cream, oil, creamed corn and 1/2 cup cheese; add to cornmeal mixture. Stir with a fork just until moistened. Spoon batter into greased muffin cups, filling 2/3 full. Top with remaining cheese. Bake at 400 degrees for about 25 minutes, until golden. Serve warm. Makes one dozen.

Lina's Taco Crackers

Lecia Stevenson
Timberville, VA

These yummy taco crackers were a gift from my sister Lina one year for Christmas. They were so good that I just had to have the recipe!

3 10-oz. pkgs. oyster crackers
3/4 c. oil
1-1/4 oz. pkg. taco seasoning
   mix

1/2 t. garlic powder
1/2 t. dried oregano
1/2 t. chili powder

Place crackers in a large roasting pan; drizzle with oil. Combine seasoning mix and spices in a small bowl; sprinkle over crackers and toss to coat. Bake, uncovered, at 350 degrees for 15 to 20 minutes, until golden, stirring once. Cool; store in an airtight container. Makes 16 cups.

Christmas Vegetable Soup

Diana Krol
Nickerson, KS

For many years this soup was served at our Methodist church's annual Christmas auction. Women from the church would each bring an ingredient, then the soup simmered all afternoon in the church kitchen. We served it with homemade French bread, followed by an assortment of homemade pies. Yum!

3 T. oil
1 meaty beef soup bone
l onion, chopped
turmeric to taste
dried thyme, sage and allspice
   to taste
1-1/2 t. salt
1/8 t. pepper

1 bay leaf
4 c. tomato juice
6 c. water
16-oz. can green beans
1 head cabbage, shredded
1 c. carrots, peeled and chopped
1 c. celery, chopped

Heat oil in a large stockpot over medium heat. Add soup bone and onion. Cook until soup bone is browned and onion is tender. Remove soup bone and set aside. Sprinkle in just enough turmeric to turn the onion yellow; stir in remaining seasonings. Cook and stir for a few minutes. Add tomato juice, water, undrained beans and vegetables. Return soup bone to pot. Cover and cook over medium-low heat for 3 to 5 hours, stirring occasionally. Remove soup bone; cut off meat and add to soup, discarding bone. Skim fat and discard bay leaf before serving. Makes 8 to 12 servings.

Don't wait 'til Christmas Day to use your festive holiday dishes... use them all season long for a daily dose of cheer!

Tuscan Turkey Soup

Alice Hardin
Antioch, CA

I love this simple soup recipe...it has become a staple for Christmas dinner when we visit our daughter and her family.

1/2 c. onion, chopped
2 cloves garlic, minced
1 lb. lean ground turkey
2 14-1/2 oz. cans chicken broth
14-1/2 oz. can diced stewed
   tomatoes
15-1/2 oz. can kidney beans,
   drained and rinsed

1/2 c. orzo pasta, uncooked
1 t. dried basil
1 t. dried oregano
1 t. salt
1/4 t. pepper
6-oz. pkg. fresh baby spinach
Garnish: shredded Parmesan
   cheese

Coat a large saucepan with non-stick vegetable spray; heat over medium heat. Add onion and garlic; sauté for 5 minutes, or just until tender. Add turkey and cook for 5 minutes. Add remaining ingredients except spinach and garnish. Bring to a boil; reduce heat, and simmer for 20 minutes, or until orzo is tender. Stir in spinach; cook for 3 minutes, or until spinach wilts. Ladle soup into bowls; top with a sprinkle of cheese. Serves 6.

Just for fun, have your Christmas cards stamped with holiday postmarks from small towns like Santa Claus, Indiana, Bethlehem, Kentucky or Rudolph, Wisconsin! Bundle stamped, addressed cards, place in a larger envelope and mail by December 15th to the postmaster at the town of your choice.

Rhonda's Taco Soup

Rhonda Hauenstein
Tell City, IN

My family has decided they like this soup better than chili! Its flavor gets even better the next day. During the wintertime we make this soup two or three times a month.

2 lbs. ground beef or turkey
1 onion, chopped
2 15-oz. cans diced tomatoes
  with garlic and onion
10-oz. can diced tomatoes with
  lime and cilantro
2 15-oz. cans seasoned pinto
  beans
15-oz. can corn, drained
2 c. tomato juice

1/4 c. brown sugar, packed
1-oz. pkg taco seasoning mix
1-oz. pkg ranch salad dressing
  mix
Optional: 4-oz. can chopped
  green chiles
Garnish: shredded Cheddar
  cheese, sour cream,
  tortilla chips

In a large stockpot over medium heat, brown meat with onion; drain. Add tomatoes with juice and remaining ingredients except garnish; stir to blend well. Cover; simmer over low heat for 45 minutes, stirring occasionally. Serve individual bowls topped with cheese, sour cream and tortilla chips. Makes 8 servings.

December is jam-packed with baking, shopping and decorating...
take it easy with simple, hearty meals. Make double batches
of family favorites like chili or Sloppy Joes early in the
holiday season and freeze half to heat and eat later.
You'll be so glad you did!

SLEDDING
Party Warmers

Potato-Leek Soup

Angela Schubbe
Saint Charles, MO

*My family loves this delicious, comforting soup for lunch
with a crisp tossed salad.*

8 potatoes, peeled and diced
2 c. chicken broth
1 white onion, diced
1 leek, white part only, diced
3 stalks celery, diced

2 T. butter
2 c. milk, warmed
2 t. sea salt, or to taste
2 t. pepper

In a large stockpot over high heat, combine potatoes and broth; cook
until tender. Meanwhile, in a separate skillet over medium heat, sauté
onion, leek and celery in butter until translucent. When potatoes are
tender, stir in onion mixture, milk and seasonings. Using a potato
masher, gently mash half of the potatoes in the stockpot to desired
texture. Warm through over low heat. Makes 9 to 12 servings.

Watch tag sales for a big red speckled enamelware stockpot...
it's just the right size for cooking up a family-size batch of soup.
The bright color adds a homey touch to any soup supper!

Fancy Pea Salad

Duane Foote
Portage, MI

I've been making this awesome side dish for at least 20 years and always get a lot of compliments. I'm 60 now and still enjoy serving this to family & friends. It's a very easy make-ahead.

2 10-oz. pkgs. frozen peas, thawed and drained
2 white onions, diced
8-oz. pkg. shredded Cheddar cheese

2 c. real bacon bits
16-oz. container sour cream
Garnish: paprika

Place peas in a large serving bowl. Add onions, cheese and bacon bits; mix well. Blend in sour cream. Sprinkle with paprika. Cover with plastic wrap. Refrigerate 2 to 3 hours, until chilled. Makes 8 to 10 servings.

Simple touches say "welcome" when family & friends visit. A snowman doormat, Christmas dishes and music playing cheerily in the background will get everyone in the holiday spirit.

Christmas Buffet Salad

Wendy Lee Paffenroth
Pine Island, NY

With green beans and red peppers, this salad is perfect for Christmas...tasty, healthy and impressive. Your guests will be surprised how simple it is to make!

3 lbs. fresh green beans, trimmed
7-oz. jar roasted red peppers,
   drained and diced
1/2 red onion, very thinly sliced

8-oz. bottle balsamic vinaigrette
   salad dressing
1/2 c. sliced black olives

Fill a large stockpot with salted water; bring to a boil over high heat. Add beans and cook for 5 minutes, or until fork-tender and bright green. Do not overcook. Drain beans; rinse with cold water and place in a large serving bowl. Add peppers and onion; mix well. Cover and refrigerate. About 30 minutes before serving time, drizzle with salad dressing; toss gently. Top with olives. Makes 12 to 14 servings.

For buffets or dinner parties, roll up flatware in colorful napkins, tie with ribbon bows and stack in a flat basket. Even kids can help...that's one less last-minute task!

Winter Cabbage Salad

Florence Coleman
Weaverville, NC

The perfect side for everything from picnics to holiday meals! This recipe has been passed along for years, and everybody likes it. You can serve it as a side salad, put it on sandwiches, use it as a relish on hot dogs and sausages. I can pretty much guarantee that if you try it, you will love it.

8 c. cabbage, finely shredded
1 red pepper, thinly sliced
1 green pepper, thinly sliced
2 onions, thinly sliced
1 c. sugar

2/3 c. vinegar
1-1/2 t. mustard seed
1 t. celery seed
1/4 t. turmeric
Optional: 1 t. salt

Combine all ingredients in a large serving bowl; toss to mix. Cover and refrigerate for one hour to overnight, stirring occasionally. Makes 12 to 14 servings.

Nothing's better on a snowy day than building a snowman!
Keep a box filled with everything the kids will need...mittens,
scarf, hat and buttons...all set for the next snowfall.

SLEDDING
Party Warmers

Cucumber Crunch Salad

Sherry Sheehan
Phoenix, AZ

This salad is very close to my grandmother's recipe. I got an idea from my friend Jill to add additional vegetables to create a lovely red and green salad that's just right with a Christmas ham.

2 cucumbers, peeled and thinly
    sliced
1 c. red pepper, diced
1 c. green pepper, diced
1 onion, sliced

1/2 c. celery, sliced
1/3 c. cider vinegar
1/3 c. water
3 T. sugar
1/2 t. salt

Combine cucumbers, peppers, onion and celery in a large bowl. In a separate small bowl, combine remaining ingredients; blend well. Pour over vegetable mixture; toss to mix. Chill for at least 2 to 3 hours before serving. Serves 8.

Fill pint-size canning jars with old-fashioned hard candies and line them up across your mantel...an instant glad-you-came gift for guests.

Festive Holiday Salad

Lena Saliba Williams
Loveland, CO

Ruby-red pomegranate seeds star in this beautiful and delicious salad.
I love to make it over the holidays when pomegranates are readily
available. Sugared almonds add a sweet touch.

3 T. sugar
1/2 c. sliced almonds
1/2 head Romaine lettuce,
    torn into bite-size pieces
1/2 head iceberg lettuce,
    torn into bite-size pieces

1 bunch green onions, chopped
1 c. celery, chopped
11-oz. can mandarin oranges,
    drained
1 pomegranate, quartered

Add sugar to a heavy skillet over medium-low heat. Cook and stir until
completely melted (sugar will be very hot). Add almonds; stir until fully
coated. Place almonds on wax paper; set aside to cool. In a large serving
bowl, combine lettuces, onions, celery and oranges; set aside. Gently
remove pomegranate seeds from rind, discarding rind and pith. Add
pomegranate seeds to salad; toss. Cover and refrigerate. Just before
serving, drizzle salad with Parsley Dressing; top with almonds.
Serves 6 to 8.

Parsley Dressing:

1/4 c. oil
1 T. fresh parsley, snipped
2 T. sugar

1/2 t. salt
1/8 t. pepper
2 T. cider vinegar

Combine all ingredients in a cruet; cover and shake well.

Vintage aprons are practical,
but also adorable! Look for the
1950s style with poinsettias,
snowmen and Santa Claus...
perfect gifts for girlfriends
who love to cook.

SLEDDING
Party Warmers

Spinach & Orange Salad

Jill Ball
Highland, UT

This is a salad I make all the time. Since oranges can be purchased year 'round, it gives you that fresh summer taste even on the coldest winter day.

10 c. fresh spinach, torn
3 oranges, peeled and sliced

1 red onion, thinly sliced and
  separated into rings

In a large salad bowl, combine spinach, oranges and onion. Pour Cilantro Dressing over salad; toss to coat. Serves 8.

Cilantro Dressing:

1/3 c. orange juice
1/3 c. cider vinegar
1/3 c. olive oil

2 T. sugar
1/4 c. fresh cilantro, chopped

In a jar with a tight-fitting lid, combine all ingredients. Shake to mix well.

A large clear glass bowl is a must for entertaining family & friends. Serve up a layered salad, a fruity punch or a sweet dessert trifle...even fill it with water and floating candles to serve as a pretty centerpiece!

Rike's Barbecue

Brenda Hager
Nancy, KY

While growing up, I often accompanied my parents to Rike's Department Store in downtown Dayton, Ohio. I looked forward to lunch on Rike's mezzanine, where I always ordered this sandwich and a cherry phosphate. Many years ago I clipped the recipe from the newspaper and have made it for my own family ever since.

2 lbs. lean ground beef
1 c. onion, chopped
1/4 c. green pepper, diced
1-1/2 c. catsup
1/4 c. sugar

1/4 c. dry mustard
2 T. cider vinegar
1 t. salt
12 sandwich buns, split

Brown beef in a skillet over medium heat; drain. Add onion and green pepper; cook for several minutes, until tender. Stir in remaining ingredients except buns. Reduce heat to low; cover and simmer until thickened, about one hour. Spoon onto buns. Serves 12.

Take a holiday photo of your family in the same place, same position each year, for example in the front of the Christmas tree...a sweet record of how the kids have grown!

Roast Beef & Herbed Cheese Sandwiches

Judi Towner
Clarks Summit, PA

These easy, delicious sandwiches are guaranteed to please any crowd! I've served them on various types of bread for ladies' bridal and baby shower luncheons...also served them on hard rolls at Super Bowl parties, and men love them too! I made them for my young grandsons, and they ate them up and asked for more. The cheese spread even makes a great dip for crackers and veggies.

8-oz. pkg. cream cheese,
   softened
1 T. lemon juice
1/2 t. garlic powder
1/2 t. dried basil
1/2 t. dill weed

1/2 t. dried parsley
1/2 t. celery salt
1/4 t. pepper
1 lb. thinly sliced deli roast beef
sliced rye bread or hard rolls

In a bowl, combine all ingredients except beef and bread. Blend well with an electric mixer on low speed until smooth. Cover and chill in refrigerator if not using immediately. To serve, spread generously on bread or rolls; top with slices of roast beef. Makes 4 sandwiches.

Wire together several jingle bells, then top with a homespun bow and a loop for hanging. Slip over your doorknob and they'll joyfully greet all your holiday guests.

Emily's All-Occasion Chicken Salad

Emily Hartzell
Portland, IN

I find this luscious chicken salad offers both comfort and celebration whenever you need them. Serve on buns, crackers, bagels or whatever strikes your fancy!

2-1/2 c. cooked chicken, diced
1 c. celery, finely chopped
1 c. seedless grapes, halved
Optional: 1 c. chopped walnuts
    or pecans

1/2 c. sweet onion, minced
3/4 c. light mayonnaise-style
    salad dressing
1 t. Worcestershire sauce
1/2 t. salt

Combine all ingredients in a large bowl. Cover and chill until serving time. Makes 4 to 6 servings.

Dress up your Christmas card envelopes with sparkly glitter pens, old-fashioned stickers and rubber stamps...each festive card is a gift of its own!

SLEDDING
Party Warmers

Turkey Swiss Club

Crystal Shook
Catawba, NC

*A perfect way to enjoy leftover turkey the day after Christmas.
Life is always better when you share!*

3 slices white bread, toasted
4 slices roast turkey
2 slices Swiss cheese
2 leaves lettuce

2 slices tomato
4 slices bacon, crisply cooked
1 T. mayonnaise

On one slice of toasted bread, layer turkey and cheese; top with another slice of bread. Add lettuce, tomato and bacon. Spread remaining bread with mayonnaise; add to sandwich. Cut in half diagonally; fasten each half with an extra-long toothpick. Serves one to 2.

Turn busy-day sandwiches into a meal with sweet potato fries... deliciously different! Slice sweet potatoes into wedges, toss with olive oil and place on a baking sheet. Bake at 400 degrees for 20 to 30 minutes, until tender, turning once. Sprinkle with a little cinnamon-sugar and serve warm.

Nannie's Banana Bread

Linda Rossworm
Ontario, Canada

My mom had a heart of gold...everyone called her Mom, not just us six kids! She taught me to bake and made it a bonding time to laugh and share memories. Although we lost her suddenly, my daughters and I bake her recipes together. I feel like she's right there with us, laughing and sharing those special times.

1 c. sugar
1/2 c. butter
2 eggs
1 c. very ripe banana, mashed
1-1/2 c. all-purpose flour

1/2 t. baking soda
1 t. baking powder
Optional: 1/2 c. chopped walnuts
Garnish: additional butter

In a large bowl, mix together all ingredients except garnish in order listed. Spoon batter into a greased 9"x5" loaf pan. Bake at 350 degrees for 45 minutes. May also be baked in 16 greased muffin cups, 20 to 25 minutes. Serve warm with butter. Makes one loaf or 16 muffins.

Place a plastic-wrapped loaf of Nannie's Banana Bread in the center of a festive, fabric napkin. Bring the corners up to the center and secure with a satiny ribbon...giftwrap couldn't be easier!

Herbed Batter Bread

Nancy Wise
Little Rock, AR

Simple to make and terrific with soup! Serve with lots of creamy butter.

1 c. onion, finely chopped
1/4 c. butter
3-1/4 c. all-purpose flour, divided
2 envs. instant dry yeast
2 T. sugar

1 t. salt
1/2 t. dried sage
1/2 t. dried rosemary
1/4 t. dried thyme
1-1/4 c. warm water
1 egg, beaten

In a skillet over medium heat, sauté onion in butter until golden. Meanwhile, in a large bowl, mix 1-1/2 cups flour, yeast, sugar, salt and herbs; set aside. Heat water until very warm, 120 to 130 degrees. Add onion mixture, water and egg to flour mixture. Beat with an electric mixer on low speed until moistened; beat at medium speed for 3 minutes. With a spoon, gradually stir in remaining flour to make a stiff batter. Spoon into a greased 2-quart round casserole dish. Cover; let rise in a warm place until double in bulk, about one hour. Bake at 375 degrees for 35 to 40 minutes, until golden. Turn bread out of dish; serve warm or cooled. Makes one loaf.

Make yourself a mug of hot cocoa, settle into a cozy corner and take time to do some of those things you've been meaning to... call old friends, sort through Mom's recipe box or read the latest holiday home magazine.

Great Blender Mustard

Carol Wambolt
Ontario, Canada

The best mustard my family has ever had! Very smooth tasting, and by altering the amount of dry mustard, you can customize it to your own liking.

1/2 c. dry mustard	2 T. white vinegar
1/2 c. sugar	1/4 c. boiling water
1/2 t. salt	1/4 c. oil
1/8 t. white pepper	1/2 c. whipping cream

Add all ingredients to a blender; process for one minute. Stir sides down and process one minute longer, or until smooth. Spoon into a jar. Cover and refrigerate for at least one day before using. Mustard will gradually improve in flavor and turn more yellow. Keep refrigerated up to 2 weeks. Makes about 2 cups.

For take-home gifts, fill Mason jars with Great Blender Mustard or your own secret sauce. Tie on a recipe card and a spreader with a bit of jute...guests will love it!

OLD-FASHIONED
Christmas Dinner

Stuffed Chicken Shells Picante

Carol Crawford
Iola, KS

My family just loves this recipe. I enjoy making it for all kinds of dinners. Speed it up with a rotisserie chicken...spice it up with the picante sauce of your choice!

16 jumbo pasta shells, uncooked
8-oz. jar picante sauce
8-oz. can tomato sauce
1/2 c. water
1-1/2 to 2 c. cooked chicken, shredded

4-oz. can chopped green chiles, drained
1-1/2 c. shredded Monterey Jack cheese, divided
3 3-oz. cans French-fried onions, divided

Cook pasta according to package directions; drain. Meanwhile, in a small bowl, combine sauces and water; mix well. Place chicken in a large bowl. Add chiles, 1/2 cup sauce mixture, 1/2 cup cheese and one can onions to chicken; mix well. Spread half of remaining sauce mixture in a 13"x9" baking pan that has been sprayed with non-stick vegetable spray. Spoon chicken mixture into cooled shells; arrange shells in baking pan. Spoon remaining sauce mixture over shells. Bake, covered, at 350 degrees for 30 minutes. Uncover; top with remaining onions and cheese. Bake an additional 5 to 8 minutes, until cheese is melted. Makes 8 servings.

A fun countdown to Christmas! Get the family together and think up 25 fun holiday activities like making gingerbread cookies for classmates, dancing to holiday music, sledding or reading a Christmas story. Write each on a calendar for December, then do the activities together.

3-Cheese Manicotti

Cindy Jamieson
Ontario, Canada

We are crazy for cheese in this house! Especially if we are having pasta. My husband taught me this tasty meatless recipe, and it's become one of our favorites.

8-oz. pkg. manicotti pasta shells, uncooked
16-oz. container ricotta cheese
1/2 c. grated Parmesan cheese
1-1/2 c. shredded mozzarella cheese, divided
1 egg, beaten

2 T. dried parsley
1/4 t. garlic powder
1/4 t. salt
1/2 t. pepper
26-oz. jar favorite pasta sauce, divided

Cook pasta according to package directions, just until tender; drain and cool. Meanwhile, mix ricotta cheese, Parmesan cheese, one cup mozzarella cheese, egg and seasonings in a bowl. Spoon mixture into a piping bag or a plastic zipping bag with one corner snipped off; fill cooled shells. Spread a thin layer of sauce in a lightly greased 13"x9" baking pan. Arrange filled shells in pan; top with remaining sauce. Sprinkle with remaining mozzarella; cover with aluminum foil. Bake at 375 degrees for 45 minutes. Remove foil; bake for an additional 15 minutes. Let stand for 10 minutes before serving. Makes 6 servings.

Turn thrift-store holiday teacups into sparkly candles...just fill with pine-scented wax chips and add a wick. Group together on a mirrored tray for extra sparkle.

Chicken & Chips Casserole

Rebecca Gonzalez
Moreno Valley, CA

My mom used to make this yummy casserole at least once a month, always on a Sunday after church. It still reminds me of my younger years and not having a care in the world.

2 c. boneless, skinless chicken
    breasts, cooked and cubed
1 c. shredded sharp Cheddar
    cheese
1 c. celery, diced
1/2 c. slivered almonds

1 c. mayonnaise
2 T. lemon juice
1/2 t. salt
1/2 t. pepper
2/3 c. potato chips, crushed

In a large bowl, combine all ingredients except potato chips. Mix well; spoon into a 13"x9" baking pan sprayed with non-stick vegetable spray. Sprinkle crushed chips on top. Bake, uncovered, at 350 degrees for 20 minutes, or until golden and bubbly. Makes 6 to 8 servings.

Traveling Treats!

Traveling home for Christmas? Take along some tiny inexpensive gifts to give the kids along the way. It helps to keep them occupied. If the children are old enough, give them a map and tell them in which towns they will receive surprises. They'll have fun keeping track.

OLD-FASHIONED
Christmas Dinner

Cheesy Ham Bake

Betty Lou Wright
Hendersonville, TN

This casserole is comforting and delicious. My family enjoys it on Christmas Eve, and it's good for brunch the next morning too...if there's any left! Sometimes for a change I use half mozzarella cheese and half Cheddar cheese.

12 slices Italian or French bread, divided
1 to 1-1/2 c. cooked ham, diced
2 c. shredded mozzarella cheese, divided

3 eggs, beaten
2 c. milk
1/4 to 1/2 c. onion, chopped
garlic salt and pepper to taste

Arrange 6 bread slices in a lightly greased 13"x9" baking pan. Sprinkle with ham and one cup cheese; top with remaining bread. In a bowl, stir together eggs, milk, onion and seasonings; pour over bread. Bake, uncovered, at 350 degrees for 40 minutes. Sprinkle with remaining cheese; bake an additional 5 minutes. Let stand 5 minutes before serving. Serves 8 to 10.

Spread out cotton batting as a snowy setting for tiny vintage houses and reindeer or snowman figures...what a sweet centerpiece! Add a dash of mica flakes for icy sparkle.

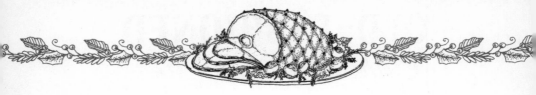

Smoked Sausage & Potato Boil

Heather Hill
Greenfield, IN

I received this recipe from a co-worker over ten years ago when I got married, and it has become one of my family's favorite go-to recipes. It requires one pot, five ingredients, 15 minutes prep time and 25 minutes to cook...pretty easy! Just add a fruit salad for a complete meal in less than an hour. The original recipe called for peeling the potatoes, but I skip that step to save time, and no one seems to mind.

1 lb. smoked pork sausage,
   cut into 2-inch pieces
4 to 6 potatoes, cubed

2 14-1/2 oz. cans green beans
4 cubes beef bouillon
Optional: catsup

Combine sausage, potatoes, undrained beans and bouillon in a stockpot. Add enough water to cover. Bring to a boil over medium-high heat. Reduce heat; cover and cook for about 25 minutes, stirring occasionally, until potatoes are tender. Serve with catsup, if desired. Serves 4 to 6.

Wire woolly mittens of all colors onto a wreath of fresh evergreen...sweet little kid-size mittens will bring back memories of Christmas past.

OLD-FASHIONED
Christmas Dinner

Lazy Pierogie

Judy Henfey
Cibolo, TX

My mother was a Christmas baby. Every Christmas morning my grandfather would come to our home and make her breakfast while the ham was baking. This hearty dish was always served with the main meal of baked ham, cabbage salad and rye bread.

32-oz. jar sauerkraut, drained and rinsed
1-1/2 c. butter, divided
1 onion, chopped
8-oz. can sliced mushrooms, drained
16-oz. pkg. rotini pasta, uncooked

Place sauerkraut in a large saucepan with a small amount of water. Cook over low heat for 30 minutes. Melt 3/4 cup butter in a skillet; sauté onion until soft. Add mushrooms, sauerkraut and remaining butter to skillet. Sauté, uncovered for 30 minutes. Meanwhile, cook pasta according to package directions, just until tender; drain. Combine sauerkraut mixture and pasta in a large serving bowl; serve. May be made ahead of time and refrigerated; reheat at 350 degrees for 30 to 45 minutes. Serves 10 to 12.

Wilted Spinach with Garlic

Regina Wickline
Pebble Beach, CA

We enjoy this fresh, simple dish with hearty holiday dinners.

2 T. olive oil
6 cloves garlic, minced
3 6-oz. pkgs. fresh baby spinach
2 t. salt
3/4 t. pepper
Garnish: butter, 1/2 lemon

Heat oil in a large skillet over medium heat. Sauté garlic for one minute, or just until lightly golden. Add spinach, salt and pepper; toss to coat. Cover and cook for 2 minutes. Uncover; increase heat to high. Cook and stir for one minute, or until wilted. Place in a serving bowl; garnish with a dollop of butter and a squeeze of lemon juice. Serves 8.

Scalloped Potatoes & Ham ▶

Jeanne Koebel
Colonie, NY

Delicious old-fashioned comfort food...our favorite way
to enjoy holiday ham leftovers!

6 T. butter, divided
1/4 c. all-purpose flour
1 t. salt
1 t. dried parsley
1/2 t. dried thyme
1 t. onion powder
3 c. milk
1 c. shredded mozzarella and/or
   Cheddar cheese

1/4 c. grated Parmesan cheese
6 to 7 potatoes, peeled, thinly
   sliced and divided
1-1/2 c. cooked ham, cubed
   and divided
10-oz. pkg. frozen corn, thawed
   and divided
1/2 c. Italian-flavored dry bread
   crumbs

In a saucepan over medium heat, melt 4 tablespoons butter. Whisk
in flour and seasonings; add milk. Bring to a boil. Cook for about
2 minutes, stirring constantly, until thickened. Remove from heat; stir
in cheeses until melted and smooth. In a greased 13"x9" baking pan,
layer half each of potatoes, ham and corn. Pour half of the cheese sauce
over top. Layer remaining potatoes, ham and corn; pour remaining
cheese sauce over top. Sprinkle with bread crumbs; dot with remaining
butter. Cover and bake at 375 degrees for about one hour, until potatoes
are tender. Uncover and bake for an additional 10 minutes, or until
bread crumbs are golden. Let stand for 10 minutes before serving.
Makes 6 servings.

Place newly arrived Christmas
cards in a vintage napkin holder,
then take a moment every
evening to share happy holiday
greetings from friends &
neighbors over dinner.

Chicken-Broccoli Piquant

Kristin Lindsey
Columbus, OH

This has been a family favorite for years! This dish can be made ahead of time, refrigerated and then baked before dinner. It also freezes well. Cubes of baked ham are a delicious substitute.

2 10-oz. pkgs. frozen broccoli
  spears
8-oz. pkg. herb-flavored stuffing
  mix
4 boneless, skinless chicken
  breasts, cooked and cubed
2 10-3/4 oz. cans regular or fat-
  free cream of mushroom soup

4-oz. can sliced mushrooms
1 c. regular or fat-free
  mayonnaise
1 t. lemon juice
1/2 t. curry powder
1/2 c. shredded sharp Cheddar
  cheese

Prepare broccoli spears and stuffing mix separately, according to package directions; set aside stuffing. Drain broccoli; arrange in a lightly greased 13"x9" baking pan. Place chicken on top. In a saucepan over medium-low heat, stir together soup, undrained mushrooms, mayonnaise, lemon juice and curry until heated through. Spoon mixture over chicken. Sprinkle with cheese; top with stuffing. Bake, uncovered, at 350 degrees for 30 minutes, or until hot and bubbly. Serves 10 to 12.

Rolls of colorful thrift-store ribbons, rick-rack and other sewing notions make the very best giftwrap trims. Place all the rolls on an upright paper towel holder for easy access.

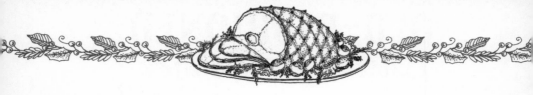

Mustard Pork Chops & Couscous

*Dale Duncan
Waterloo, IA*

*Savory pork chops with their own side dish...just add a
steamed vegetable and dinner is served!*

4 thick pork chops, butterflied
2 T. Dijon mustard
4 t. lime juice
2 t. ground cumin

2 c. couscous, uncooked
2 c. chicken broth
2 T. butter, sliced

Line a broiler pan with aluminum foil; spray lightly with non-stick
vegetable spray. Arrange pork chops on pan; set aside. In a small bowl,
whisk together mustard, lime juice and cumin. Brush half of mixture
over chops. Broil, 2 inches from heat, for 5 minutes. Turn chops over;
brush with remaining mustard mixture. Broil for an additional
5 minutes, or until no longer pink in the center. Meanwhile, prepare
couscous according to package directions, using broth instead of water.
Dot couscous with butter; serve with chops. Serves 4.

With houses decorated for the holidays, it's a great time to hold
a progressive dinner! Each family serves one course at their house
as everyone travels from home to home. Begin at one house for
appetizers, move to the next for soup and salad, again for the
main dish and end with dessert. It's all about food & fun!

Greek Pork Loin

Andrea Treadwell
Orrington, ME

We created this recipe after tasting a similar one at a dinner party. It's incredible and so easy! Scrumptious served on a bed of rice or noodles.

2-lb. pork tenderloin
14-1/2 oz. can diced tomatoes
    with garlic and onions
4-oz. can sliced black olives,
    drained

1/2 to 3/4 c. crumbled feta
    cheese

Place tenderloin in a lightly greased 13"x9" baking pan. Pour tomatoes with juice and olives over top. Sprinkle with feta cheese. Bake, uncovered, at 350 degrees for about one hour, until no longer pink in the center. Makes 6 to 8 servings.

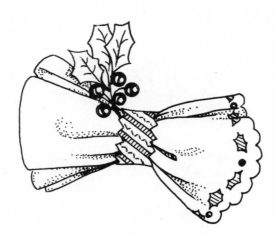

Turn Christmas cards into festive napkin rings. Cut them into wide strips with decorative-edge scissors, join ends with craft glue and add a sprig of faux holly...simple!

Glazed Pork Roast

Cathy Hillier
Salt Lake City, UT

Our favorite holiday dinner! Years ago Mom would use the little round spiced crabapples you could buy in jars...we kids loved them. They're hard to find now, but the spiced apple rings are good too.

4-lb. boneless pork roast
14-1/2 oz. jar spiced apple rings,
   drained and juice reserved

1 T. lemon juice
1/3 c. brown sugar, packed

Place roast, fat-side up, on a rack in a roasting pan. Do not add any water. Bake, uncovered, at 325 degrees for one hour and 20 to 30 minutes, until a meat thermometer inserted in the center reads 160 degrees. While roast is baking, combine reserved apple juice, lemon juice and brown sugar in a saucepan. Cook over low heat, stirring often, for 5 to 8 minutes, until slightly thickened. Brush juice mixture over roast 2 to 3 times during final 30 minutes of baking time. Let roast stand several minutes before slicing. Serve slices on a platter, surrounded with apples. Makes 6 servings.

The secret of the best Christmases is everybody
doing the same things all at the same time.
–Robert P. Tristram Coffin

OLD-FASHIONED
Christmas Dinner

Santa's Beef Tenderloin Deluxe

Elizabeth Conroy-Powers
Rochester, MI

Twenty years ago I tried this recipe, wanting to make a memorable Christmas dinner for my family. It's been requested ever since!

2-lb. beef tenderloin
4 T. butter, softened and divided
1 lb. sliced mushrooms
1/4 c. green onions, chopped
3/4 c. dry sherry or beef broth

2 T. soy sauce
1 t. Dijon mustard
1/8 t. coarse pepper
Optional: 1/4 t. cornstarch

Spread tenderloin with 2 tablespoons butter. Place on a rack in a shallow roasting pan. Bake, uncovered, at 400 degrees, 40 minutes for medium-rare or 50 minutes for medium. In a skillet over medium heat, sauté mushrooms and onions in remaining butter. Add remaining ingredients, using cornstarch if a thicker sauce is desired. Cook and stir until boiling. Let tenderloin stand for several minutes; slice and serve with sauce. Serves 4 to 6.

Onion Yorkshire Pudding

Melissa Knight
Athens, AL

This is the best side dish for any Christmas dinner! It goes well with just about any roast...beef, pork, chicken or ham.

1 onion, sliced
2 T. butter
2 t. salt, divided
1 t. pepper

3/4 c. plus 2 T. all-purpose flour
2 eggs, beaten
3/4 c. water
3/4 c. milk

In a cast-iron skillet over medium-high heat, sauté onion in butter until tender and golden. Add one teaspoon salt and pepper; spoon into an ungreased 9" pie plate. In a large bowl, combine flour and remaining salt. In a separate bowl, whisk together eggs, water and milk; add to flour mixture and whisk until just blended. Pour batter over onion mixture. Bake, uncovered, at 400 degrees for 30 to 35 minutes, until golden. Cut into wedges; serve warm. Serves 6 to 8.

Tender Turkey Breast

Deanna Polito-Laughinghouse
Knightdale, NC

The most flavorful, moist turkey breast you'll ever taste! I serve this on Christmas for my family, and the reviews are always amazing.

4-lb. turkey breast, thawed if
    frozen
2 T. olive oil
2 t. garlic powder
2 t. dried oregano

2 t. Italian seasoning
2 t. seasoned salt
2 t. salt
2 t. pepper
14-1/2 oz. can chicken broth

Place turkey breast in a lightly greased 13"x9" baking pan; brush lightly with oil. Mix seasonings in a small bowl; rub over turkey. Add broth to pan. Bake, uncovered, at 325 degrees for 1-1/2 to 2-1/4 hours. Remove from oven; let stand in pan at least 10 minutes, or until broth is partially absorbed. Slice; serve drizzled with remaining broth from pan. Makes 6 to 8 servings.

Grandma's Cranberry Salad

Becky Kuchenbecker
Ravenna, OH

Grandma Gless made this tasty no-cook cranberry salad every Thanksgiving and Christmas. My mother has carried on the tradition...it wouldn't be a holiday without it!

4 c. fresh cranberries
1 apple, quartered and cored
1 orange, quartered

1/2 c. celery, chopped
Optional: 1/2 c. chopped pecans
1 to 1-1/2 c. sugar

In a food processor, grind cranberries, apple and orange, including peel, to desired consistency. Transfer to a bowl; add celery and pecans, if using. Add sugar to taste; mix well. Cover and refrigerate 8 hours to overnight before serving. Makes 8 servings.

Play holiday music quietly during family dinners...try jazz, contemporary and country themes and find your family's favorites.

Sweetie's Dressing

Patricia Buchanan
Columbia, MO

Everyone called Mom "Sweetie" which she certainly was. There are a lot of great cooks, but our Sweetie was the best. She didn't use a recipe very often...she just made it up as she went. This is our best rendition of her delicious dressing that we enjoyed every holiday.

1/2 c. onion, chopped
1/2 c. celery, chopped
1 to 2 T. butter
1-1/2 loaves white bread,
   cubed and dried
3 14-oz. cans chicken broth

10-3/4 oz. can cream of celery
   soup
4 eggs, beaten
2 t. dried sage
1 t. dried parsley
salt and pepper to taste

In a skillet over medium heat, sauté onion and celery in butter. Transfer onion mixture to a very large bowl; add remaining ingredients and toss to mix. Spread in a lightly greased 13"x9" baking pan. Bake, uncovered, at 375 degrees for one hour and 15 minutes. Serves 10 to 12.

Gather the children together on Christmas Eve and snuggle under quilts or in sleeping bags around the tree. Turn on the tree lights and light some candles...read *'Twas the Night Before Christmas* with mugs of hot cocoa to sip. Memories in the making!

Mom's Beef Stroganoff

Jennie Gist
Gooseberry Patch

This recipe has always been Mom's special-occasion recipe, but the tomato-based sauce is a little different from the usual brown gravy. Both my brother Dan and my sister Linda were surprised to find out that stroganoff meant something different to their spouses. It's delicious, so I hope you give it a try!

2 lbs. beef round steak, sliced
    into thin strips
1/2 c. all-purpose flour
3 to 4 T. oil
28-oz. can tomato purée
12-oz. can tomato paste

2 6-oz. jars sliced mushrooms,
    drained
salt and pepper to taste
16-oz. container sour cream
16-oz. pkg. wide egg noodles,
    uncooked

In a shallow bowl, coat beef strips in flour. Heat oil in a stockpot over medium-high heat and brown strips on all sides. Drain; stir in tomato purée, tomato paste and mushrooms. Season with salt and pepper. Reduce heat to low; cover and simmer until beef is tender, about 45 minutes. Meanwhile, cook noodles according to package directions; drain. When beef is tender, remove pot from heat; stir in sour cream. To serve, ladle beef and sauce over noodles. Serves 6.

Make time for your town's special holiday events. Whether it's a Christmas parade, Santa arriving by horse-drawn sleigh or a tree lighting ceremony, hometown traditions make the best memories!

OLD-FASHIONED
Christmas Dinner

Braised Beef Short Ribs

Marcia Shaffer
Conneaut Lake, PA

This recipe has been handed down in my family since 1940s. It's so simple to make and is always a hit.

1-1/4 c. all-purpose flour
salt and pepper to taste
3 lbs. beef short ribs, cut into
    serving-size portions
1/4 c. oil

1 onion, thinly sliced
1/2 c. water
2 T. catsup
1 T. vinegar
1/4 t. dried thyme

Mix flour, salt and pepper in a shallow bowl. Dredge ribs in flour mixture. Brown ribs in oil in a heavy skillet over medium-high heat. Drain, reserving drippings in skillet. Remove ribs to an ungreased 3-quart casserole dish. Add remaining ingredients to drippings; stir until well blended and hot. Pour over ribs. Bake, uncovered, at 325 degrees for 2 hours, until very tender. Serves 4 to 5.

Hosting a dinner party for family & friends? Hang a homespun stocking filled with goodies on the back of each chair for instant country charm!

Mama's Chicken Pot Pies

Yvette Garza
Livingston, CA

Mmm...made-from-scratch pot pies! I bake all of the pies, then wrap, freeze and label six of them. They're wonderful for busy-day dinners and are sure to be welcomed as gifts too. To serve, unwrap pie and bake at 400 degrees for 45 to 60 minutes, until bubbly and golden.

8 boneless, skinless chicken
   breasts
8 to 10 c. water
1-1/2 t. garlic salt
1-1/2 c. margarine
3 onions, chopped
1-1/2 c. biscuit baking mix
9 stalks celery, chopped

9 potatoes, peeled and diced
10-oz. pkg. green beans, frozen
10-oz. pkg. corn, frozen
1-1/2 t. salt
1-1/2 t. pepper
additional garlic salt to taste
16 9-inch pie crusts

Place chicken, water and garlic salt in a large stockpot over medium-high heat. Bring to a boil; reduce heat to low. Cover and simmer for 30 to 45 minutes, until chicken juices run clear when pierced. Remove chicken to a bowl, reserving 7-1/2 cups of broth in stockpot. Cool and shred chicken. Meanwhile, in a separate large saucepan, melt margarine over medium heat; stir in onions and baking mix. Cook and stir until bubbly; remove from heat. Bring reserved broth to a boil; add onion mixture and remaining vegetables. Boil for one minute, stirring constantly. Add chicken and seasonings; simmer over low heat until vegetables are tender, 15 to 20 minutes. Arrange 8 pie crusts in 9" pie plates; fill evenly with chicken mixture. Top with remaining crusts; crimp edges and cut slits in top crusts to vent. Cover oven racks with aluminum foil to catch any drips. Bake pies at 400 degrees for 40 to 45 minutes, until bubbly and crusts are golden. Let stand 10 minutes before serving. Makes 8 pot pies; each serves 4.

If you're planning to string popcorn as a tree garland, pop it a couple days before you plan to string it and it will hold up nicely.

OLD-FASHIONED
Christmas Dinner

Turkey Scallop

Bethanna Kortie
Greer, SC

I inherited my husband's mother's cookbook, filled with old-fashioned handwritten recipes from his mother, grandmother and great-grandmother! I adapted this dish from one grandmotherly recipe. It's a wonderful way to enjoy holiday leftovers.

2-1/2 c. seasoned croutons
1/2 c. butter, melted and divided
1 c. celery, diced
1/2 c. chicken broth

1-1/2 c. milk
1/4 c. all-purpose flour
1 c. roast turkey, diced
Garnish: fresh parsley

In a bowl, drizzle croutons with 1/4 cup melted butter; toss to coat and set aside. In a saucepan over medium heat, cook celery in broth until tender. Drain; pour broth into a 2-cup glass measuring cup. Add enough milk to broth to make 2 cups. In the same saucepan, stir flour into remaining melted butter. Gradually add reserved broth mixture. Cook until thickened, stirring constantly. Arrange half of croutons in an ungreased 1-1/2 quart casserole dish. Top with turkey, celery and remaining croutons; pour sauce over top. Bake, uncovered, at 350 degrees until heated through, 20 to 25 minutes. Garnish with parsley. Makes 4 servings.

Don't toss out that little bit of leftover cranberry sauce! Purée it with balsamic vinaigrette to create a tangy salad dressing that's perfect over crisp greens and fruit.

Inside-Out Raviolis

Randi Buckley
Rochester, NY

*Every fall after the first snowfall, my children and I gather around
our large kitchen table and make these yummy raviolis.*

1 lb. ground beef
1 onion
1 c. catsup
1 c. sugar
1/4 c. soy sauce
3 c. water
12-oz. pkg. lasagna noodles,
    uncooked and broken into
    small pieces

14-1/2 oz. can stewed tomatoes
10-3/4 oz. can tomato soup
1 T. oil
2 t. dried parsley
1 t. paprika
1 t. garlic powder
2 bay leaves

In a skillet over medium heat, brown beef and onion; drain. Stir in
catsup, sugar and soy sauce; bring to a boil. Remove from heat and set
aside. Meanwhile, in a large saucepan, bring water to a boil over high
heat; add lasagna. Boil for 12 minutes, stirring constantly to avoid
sticking. Stir in tomatoes in juice, soup and oil. Reduce to medium-low
heat; cover and simmer for 35 minutes. Add beef mixture and
seasonings to lasagna mixture; simmer over high heat for 10 minutes.
Remove from heat; discard bay leaves. Let stand for 15 minutes before
serving. Serves 6.

Wrap your front door like a giant gift box! It's easy with a plastic
party tablecloth and clear tape. Add a big ribbon bow and an
oversized gift tag with a cheerful message.

OLD-FASHIONED
Christmas Dinner

Zesty Italian Chicken Pasta

Tawnia Hultink
Ontario, Canada

My friend Kendra shared this recipe with us. It truly is so easy and tastes like you went to a delicious Italian restaurant. Oh, the flavor is wonderful! You can also use peeled shrimp instead of chicken.

9-oz. pkg. favorite pasta, uncooked
1 lb. boneless, skinless chicken breasts, cut into strips
3/4 c. zesty Italian salad dressing, divided
14-oz. can artichoke hearts, drained and halved
1/2 c. onion, chopped
1 T. fresh parsley, snipped
Optional: 2 c. sliced mushrooms
1/4 c. grated Parmesan cheese
Optional: 2 T. pine nuts, lightly toasted

Cook pasta according to package directions; drain. Meanwhile, in a large skillet over medium-high heat, cook and stir chicken in 1/2 cup salad dressing for 4 to 5 minutes. Add artichokes, onion, parsley and mushrooms, if using. Cook until vegetables are tender, stirring frequently. Toss with cooked pasta and remaining salad dressing. Sprinkle with Parmesan cheese and pine nuts, if using. Serves 6.

Host a tree-trimming party. Invite all the cousins, aunts & uncles for a merry time hanging ornaments and twining garland...even set up a table of craft materials so guests can make their own. Afterwards, share holiday plans over a simple supper. Such fun!

Italian Fish Skillet

Mia Rossi
Charlotte, NC

A super-simple dish for a busy shopping day.

14-1/2 oz. can Italian-style
  stewed tomatoes
1/4 c. sliced black olives

1-1/2 lbs. haddock fillets
1/8 t. pepper
Garnish: grated Parmesan cheese

Add tomatoes with juice to a skillet. Simmer over medium heat for about 5 minutes, until most of juice has evaporated. Stir in olives. Arrange fish in skillet in a single layer; sprinkle with pepper. Cover and cook over medium heat for 5 to 7 minutes, until fish flakes easily with a fork. Serve fish with tomato mixture spooned over top; sprinkle with Parmesan cheese. Serves 4.

Baked Ranch Potatoes

Pat Martin
Riverside, CA

Some of our family members don't eat dairy products, so they can't enjoy our holiday potato-cheese casserole. For them, I created this tasty potato recipe. It was such a hit that the whole family eats it.

8 large redskin potatoes
1/4 c. olive oil

1-oz. pkg ranch salad dressing
  mix

Up to a day ahead, place whole potatoes in a microwave-safe dish. Microwave on high for 5 to 7 minutes, until partially cooked. Refrigerate potatoes if not using immediately. Dice potatoes and return to dish. Add oil and dressing mix; toss to coat. Spread in a single layer on a greased baking sheet. Bake at 400 degrees for 30 to 40 minutes, turning once, until crisp and golden. Serves 6 to 8.

OLD-FASHIONED
Christmas Dinner

Lemony Baked Fish & Potatoes

JoAnn

My family likes this light one-pan meal...it means they have more room for Christmas cookies afterwards!

1/2 c. butter, melted
2 cloves garlic, minced
3 T. lemon juice
2 t. lemon zest
3/4 t. garlic pepper

1 T. fresh dill, chopped
salt and pepper to taste
3/4 lb. redskin potatoes, quartered
1 lb. tilapia fillets

In a small bowl, blend together butter, garlic, juice, zest and garlic pepper. Reserve 3 tablespoons of mixture. In a bowl, combine remaining butter mixture, dill, salt and pepper; add potatoes and toss to coat. Place potatoes on a lightly greased 15"x10" jelly-roll pan. Bake at 400 degrees for 30 minutes, stirring several times. Push potatoes to one end of pan; arrange fish on pan. Spoon reserved butter mixture over fish. Bake for 10 to 15 minutes, until fish flakes easily with a fork and potatoes are tender and golden. Serves 4.

Skillet Green Beans

Jen Thomas
Santa Rosa, CA

A fresh, tasty side that's red and green for Christmas

2 to 3 slices bacon
1 onion, chopped
1 lb. fresh green beans, trimmed and cut into 2-inch pieces

1/2 c. chicken broth
1/4 t. pepper
4 roma tomatoes, chopped

In a skillet over medium heat, cook bacon until crisp. Remove bacon to a paper towel, reserving drippings in skillet. Add onion to drippings; cook and stir until crisp-tender. Add beans, broth and pepper; stir. Bring to a boil. Cover and simmer over medium-low heat for 4 minutes. Stir in tomatoes; heat through. Top with crumbled bacon. Makes 6 servings.

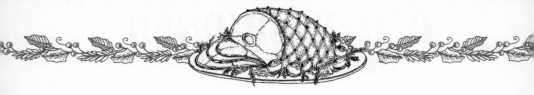

Balsamic Vinegar-Glazed Carrots

Rachel Boyd
Defiance, OH

This is a hit for holiday gatherings! My brother-in-law told me that he and his daughter loved carrots, but they hadn't found a carrot recipe they really liked until I created this one.

1 lb. baby carrots
3 T. butter, melted
2 T. brown sugar, packed

1/2 t. ground ginger
1 t. white balsamic vinegar

Cover carrots with water in a saucepan. Cook over medium-high heat until tender; drain. Whisk together remaining ingredients in a bowl; pour over carrots and toss to coat. Holds well in a warm oven until serving time. Serves 4 to 6.

Orange-Glazed Beets

Sandy Ann Ward
Anderson, IN

Grandma found this recipe on a can label many years ago. It's still a winner in our family!

16-oz. can cut beets
1 T. butter
2 t. all-purpose flour

2 T. brown sugar, packed
1/2 c. orange juice

Pour beets and their liquid into a saucepan. Heat over medium heat; drain and keep warm. In a separate small saucepan, melt butter over medium-low heat. Remove from heat; whisk in flour. Add brown sugar and orange juice. Return to heat; stir constantly until thickened. Add sauce to beets; stir to coat. Serves 4 to 6.

Mini houses look sweet lined up across a mantel. Dress them up for winter with colored lights, tinsel garland, button doorknobs and tiny trees.

OLD-FASHIONED
Christmas Dinner

Orange Curried Rice

Carolyn Moran
Centerville, OH

Easy enough for everyday meals...tasty enough for company! This side dish goes especially well with roast chicken or baked ham.

1/2 c. onion, chopped
1/4 c. butter
2 t. curry powder
1 c. long-cooking rice, uncooked
1 c. orange juice

1 c. chicken broth
1/2 c. regular or golden raisins
1 t. salt
1 bay leaf

In a heavy saucepan over medium heat, sauté onion in butter until translucent. Stir in curry powder and uncooked rice; cook and stir 2 minutes, or until rice is golden. Add remaining ingredients; stir with a fork. Bring to a boil; reduce heat to medium-low. Cover and simmer for 20 minutes, or until rice is tender. Remove bay leaf before serving. Makes 6 servings.

It's fun to hang little unexpected surprises from the dining room chandelier. Start with a swag of greenery, then tuck in Christmas whimsies like glass balls, tiny snowmen, cookie cutters and smiling Santas.

Bacon & Cheese Party Potatoes

Shelley Turner
Boise, ID

Coming from Idaho, I know my potatoes! Loaded with sour cream, bacon and two kinds of cheese, these spuds are spectacular.

4 c. mashed potatoes
1/2 c. sour cream
1/4 c. onion, chopped
1 clove garlic, minced
1-1/2 c. shredded Cheddar
   cheese
1 c. grated Parmesan cheese,
   divided

1/2 lb. bacon, crisply cooked,
   crumbled and divided
1/2 t. salt
1/4 t. pepper
1 c. dry bread crumbs
1/4 c. butter, melted

In a large bowl, combine mashed potatoes, sour cream, onion, garlic and Cheddar cheese. Add 3/4 cup Parmesan cheese and 3/4 of the bacon. Season with salt and pepper; mix well. Spread in a greased 3-quart casserole dish. Mix remaining Parmesan cheese and bacon with bread crumbs; add melted butter and toss to coat well. Sprinkle mixture over potatoes. Bake, uncovered, at 350 degrees for about 30 minutes, until heated through and topping is golden. Serves 8.

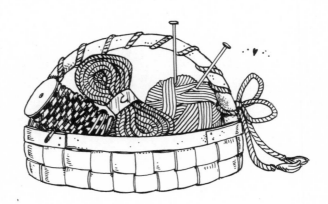

No more ordinary ribbon! A hometown knitting shop is sure to have yarns in lots of exciting colors and textures that will make gifts stand out under the tree. Bulky yarns are perfect... thin yarns can be doubled or tripled.

Horseradish Potatoes

Phyllis Broich-Wessling
Garner, IA

*Who doesn't love mashed potatoes? These flavorful potatoes
really jazz up any simple meal.*

4 to 5 redskin potatoes
1 c. sour cream
2 T. prepared horseradish

1 t. dried basil
2 T. butter, softened
salt and pepper to taste

Cut unpeeled potatoes into halves or quarters, depending on size of
potatoes. Cover with water in a saucepan. Cook over medium-high heat
until soft enough to mash, 15 to 20 minutes. Drain; mash with
remaining ingredients, leaving potatoes chunky. Serves 4 to 6.

Show off three or four of your family's most treasured Christmas
ornaments...hang them on a countertop coffee mug holder.
Finish with a few twists of tinsel.

Nanny's Blue Cheese Potatoes

Peggy Pelfrey
Ashland City, TN

This is a recipe that my Nanny made when I was little. We would always take it with us to church socials...everyone requested these scrumptious potatoes from her! The recipe feeds a crowd but is easy to divide. Yum yum!

16 potatoes, peeled and cubed
1 c. butter
1 c. all-purpose flour
2 c. milk

2 c. whipping cream
1 c. crumbled blue cheese
2/3 c. Italian-flavored dry
    bread crumbs

Place potatoes in a large saucepan; add enough water to cover. Bring to a boil over medium-high heat and cook until tender, about 10 to 15 minutes. Drain; transfer to a lightly greased 3-quart casserole dish and set aside. Melt butter in a medium saucepan over medium-high heat. Whisk in flour and cook for 5 minutes, stirring constantly. Gradually whisk in milk and cream until smooth. Reduce heat and simmer for 20 minutes; remove from heat. Whisk in blue cheese until smooth. Pour mixture over potatoes; sprinkle with bread crumbs. Bake, uncovered, at 375 degrees for 25 minutes, or until top is golden. Serves 12.

Tie on your prettiest Christmas apron and invite family & friends to join you in the kitchen to whip up a favorite dish. Everyone loves to pitch in, and it's a fun way to catch up on holiday plans.

Orelia's Squash Casserole

Rebecca Mosher
Crossett, AR

My husband is a minister. At his first preaching position, when we were invited to one of the elders' homes for dinner for the first time, the elder's wife served us a dish that looked wonderful. After I took a helping, I asked what it was and she said "Squash Casserole." I thought, "Oh no! I hate squash!" But it turned out to be a wonderful recipe, and I've been making it ever since...20 years now.

5 to 6 c. yellow squash, cubed
1 onion, chopped
8-oz. container sour cream
2 c. shredded Cheddar cheese

6-oz. pkg. herb-flavored stuffing
   mix
1/2 c. margarine, melted

Cover squash and onion with water in a large saucepan. Cook over medium-high heat until tender, about 10 minutes; drain. Stir in sour cream and cheese; set aside. In a bowl, drizzle dry stuffing mix with melted margarine; toss to mix. Reserve stuffing seasoning packet for another use. Spoon 1/3 of stuffing mixture into a lightly greased 2-quart casserole dish. Top with squash mixture; add remaining stuffing mixture. Cover and bake at 350 degrees for 15 to 20 minutes. Uncover and bake an additional 5 to 10 minutes, until top is lightly golden. Makes 6 to 8 servings.

Be sure to share family stories behind the special dishes that are a tradition at every holiday dinner. There may even be stories to tell about your vintage tablecloth or the whimsical salt & pepper shakers!

Friendship Sweet Potato Bake

Judy Henfey
Cibolo, TX

I'm a registered nurse and have worked often on Christmas. When my husband was serving in the US Air Force, we lived far away from family. During one of our first holidays alone, I found myself having to work and prepare the Christmas dinner for my husband and small son, which I had never done before. My co-worker Vernann took me under her wing. During lunch breaks, she would share quick holiday cooking tips with me and helped me plan my dinner. One day she shared her family's prized sweet potato recipe with me! Her friendship has always been one of my greatest Christmas gifts. This recipe can easily be prepared a day ahead.

3 c. sweet potatoes, peeled and
    cubed
3/4 c. sugar
1/2 c. butter, softened

2 eggs, beaten
1 t. vanilla extract
1/2 to 3/4 c. milk

Cover sweet potatoes with water in a large saucepan. Cook over medium-high heat until tender, 15 to 20 minutes. Drain; cool slightly. Add remaining ingredients and mash until well combined, adding milk to desired consistency. Spoon mixture into a lightly greased 2-quart casserole dish. Sprinkle Pecan Topping over potatoes. Bake, uncovered, at 375 degrees for 20 to 30 minutes. Serves 6 to 8.

Pecan Topping:

1 c. brown sugar, packed
1/3 c. all-purpose flour

1 c. chopped pecans
3/4 c. butter, softened

Combine brown sugar, flour and chopped pecans with a fork. Mix well. Add butter; mix until crumbly.

Be sure to have take-out containers
on hand to send guests home with
leftovers...if there are any!

OLD-FASHIONED
Christmas Dinner

Fruit-Stuffed Acorn Squash

Arden Regnier
East Moriches, NY

Grandma and I loved acorn squash, so as soon as it was in season, she would make this dish for the two of us.

1 acorn squash, halved or
    quartered and seeds removed
1 apple, peeled, cored and diced
1/4 c. raisins or sweetened dried
    cranberries

brown sugar, honey or maple
    syrup to taste
2 T. butter, sliced
cinnamon and nutmeg to taste

Place squash pieces cut-side up in an ungreased 9"x9" baking pan. Fill squash evenly with fruit; top with desired amount of brown sugar, honey or maple syrup. Dot with butter. Sprinkle with spices. Bake, uncovered, at 350 degrees for about 45 minutes, or until tender. Serves 2 to 4.

Is the whole family coming for a holiday meal? Copy one of Grandma's tried & true recipes onto a festive card, then punch a hole in the corner and tie the card to a napkin with a length of ribbon...a sweet keepsake.

Taste of the Holidays Relish

Bethi Hendrickson
Danville, PA

This jam has become a most-requested favorite among my family & friends. It makes an excellent gift for the holidays, and turns a cold turkey sandwich into something special.

5 c. fresh cranberries
2 c. water
1/2 c. chopped walnuts, toasted
1 orange, unpeeled and chopped
1 apple, cored and chopped
1-3/4 oz. pkg. powdered fruit
    pectin

1/2 t. butter
4-1/2 c. sugar
7 1/2-pint canning jars
    and lids, sterilized

Place cranberries and water in a large saucepan. Bring to a boil over medium heat. Reduce heat to low; cover and simmer for 10 minutes. Add walnuts, orange, apple, pectin and butter; stir and bring to a boil. Add sugar and bring to a rolling boil; boil for one minute, stirring constantly. Ladle into hot sterilized jars, leaving 1/4-inch headspace. Wipe rims; secure with lids and rings. Process in a boiling-water bath for 20 minutes. Set jars on a towel to cool. Check for seals. Makes 7 half-pint jars.

Homemade jam or relish is always a welcome gift! Dress up jars with a topper of colorful fabric. Cut out a circle of fabric 2 inches larger than the jar lid, place fabric over lid and secure with ribbon or jute. Charming, and so simple to do.

OPEN HOUSE...
You're Invited!

Gramma Allotta's Fried Ravioli

Edna Allotta
San Antonio, TX

This appetizer is still a hit after 40 years! Every Christmas Eve my husband and our boys have celebrated the same way, with a "Feast of the Seven Fishes" and one fish dish for each of the Seven Sacraments. Many Italian families do this. We eat everything from shrimp, scallops and tuna to oysters and whatever else may be available at the fish market. We add pasta dishes to highlight the many flavors of the fish. My boys have always loved this appetizer, which could not be simpler.

5 eggs
24-oz. pkg. Italian-flavored dry
   bread crumbs
2 to 3 lbs. frozen cheese ravioli

1/2 gal. canola oil
Garnish: marinara sauce,
   Alfredo sauce

Beat eggs in a shallow dish; place crumbs in a separate shallow dish. Dip frozen ravioli into egg, then into bread crumbs. Place ravioli on a large platter and let stand 5 minutes. In a large deep saucepan, heat oil to 365 degrees over medium-high heat. Add ravioli, no more than 8 at a time; fry until golden. Drain on paper towels. While ravioli are frying, warm sauces. Serve hot ravioli on a platter with small bowls of sauces for dipping. Serves 10.

Be sure to ask your children about their favorite foods for the Christmas season. You may find you have "traditions" in your own family that you weren't even aware of!

OPEN HOUSE...
You're Invited!

Brande's Artichoke Fingers

Brande Grieder
Glen Gardner, NJ

We have a New Year's Day brunch every year...this yummy appetizer is always on the menu.

2-1/2 c. shredded Cheddar
   cheese
2 6-oz. jars marinated artichoke
   hearts, drained and chopped
4 eggs, beaten

1/3 c. green onions, minced
8 unsalted saltine crackers,
   crushed
1-1/4 oz. pkg. ranch salad
   dressing mix

Combine all ingredients in a large bowl; stir until well mixed. Pour mixture into a buttered 8"x8" baking pan. Bake at 350 degrees for 20 to 25 minutes. Let stand for 20 minutes; cut into rectangles. Serves 9.

Make holiday entertaining extra easy with an all-appetizer party...
extra tasty too! Set up tables in different areas so guests can
mingle as they enjoy yummy finger foods. Your party is
sure to be a festive success!

Crowd-Pleasin' Chutney Spread

Gina McClenning
Brooksville, FL

Why is it that anything with bacon in it is so darn good? This is one of those spreads that is always a hit at parties!

2 8-oz. pkgs. light cream cheese, softened
3 T. curry powder
1 t. salt
5-oz. jar ginger chutney or other favorite chutney

2 bunches green onions, sliced
10 slices bacon, crisply cooked and crumbled
1/4 c. almonds, finely chopped
Melba toast or wheat crackers

In a bowl, combine cream cheese and seasonings. Blend well; spread in the bottom of a 10" quiche dish. Purée chutney in a food processor or blender. Spread chutney over cheese mixture. Sprinkle evenly with onions, bacon and almonds. Serve immediately, or cover and refrigerate up to a day ahead. Serve with Melba toast or wheat crackers. Serves 8.

Trim a doll-size Christmas tree with mini ornaments...it's just the right size for a holiday buffet table. So sweet!

OPEN HOUSE...
You're Invited!

Cranberry-Pecan Spread

Jennifer Holbrook
Manchester, MD

*I like to give this scrumptious spread a festive look
with a sprig of holly leaves and berries.*

8-oz. pkg. cream cheese,
  softened
2 T. frozen orange juice
  concentrate, thawed
1 T. sugar
2 t. orange zest

1/8 t. cinnamon
1/4 c. sweetened dried
  cranberries, finely chopped
1/4 c. pecans, finely chopped
assorted crackers

In a bowl, combine cream cheese, orange juice, sugar, zest and
cinnamon. Beat with an electric mixer on medium speed until fluffy. Stir
in cranberries and pecans. Cover and refrigerate at least one hour. Serve
with assorted crackers. Makes 1-1/2 cups.

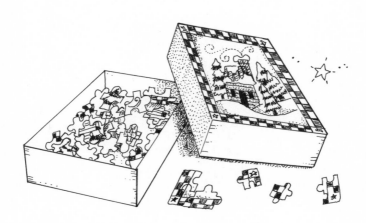

Lay out a Christmas-themed jigsaw puzzle on a table near the
fireplace...party guests are sure to enjoy fitting a few pieces
into place as they relax with a plateful of appetizers.

Mimi's Blue Cheese Dip

Jennifer Trinkle
Newport News, VA

My grandmother, fondly known as Mimi, passed away just before Christmas of 2011. This was one of the recipes she was known for, and it was often requested at family gatherings.

16-oz. container sour cream
8-oz. pkg. cream cheese,
  softened
4-oz. container crumbled
  blue cheese
1/4 c. onion, finely chopped

1/2 to 3/4 c. mayonnaise
Worcestershire sauce to taste
hot pepper sauce to taste
garlic salt to taste
sliced vegetables, crackers
  or bread

In a large bowl, blend together sour cream, cheeses and onion. Add mayonnaise to desired consistency. Season with sauces and garlic salt. Cover and chill at least 2 hours to allow flavors to blend. Serve with vegetables, crackers or bread. Makes about 3-1/2 cups.

Have an appetizer swap with three or four girlfriends! Each makes a big batch of her favorite dip, spread or finger food, then get together to sample and divide 'em up. You'll all have a super variety of goodies for holiday parties.

OPEN HOUSE...
You're Invited!

Perfect Pimento Cheese

Tina Goodpasture
Meadowview, VA

Delicious and easy to make...the best pimento cheese ever!

8-oz. pkg. shredded sharp
   Cheddar cheese
8-oz. pkg. shredded mild
   Cheddar cheese

1/2 c. cream cheese, softened
2-oz. jar diced pimentos, drained
1/2 to 3/4 c. mayonnaise

Mix together cream cheeses and pimentos in a bowl. Stir in enough mayonnaise to make a creamy consistency. Makes about 4 cups.

Creamy Beef Spread

Kathy Oberst
Okeene, OK

This is a game-day staple at our house...my boys love it!
It's delicious on crunchy crackers.

8-oz. pkg. cream cheese,
   softened
1/4 c. sour cream
1/4 c. mayonnaise

1/4 c. grated Parmesan cheese
1 green onion, finely chopped
2-1/2 oz. jar dried beef, finely
   chopped and divided

In a bowl, beat cream cheese until smooth. Add remaining ingredients, reserving 2 tablespoons dried beef. Mix well and transfer to a small serving bowl; sprinkle with reserved beef. Cover and refrigerate until serving time. Makes 1-1/2 cups.

Fill a Mason jar with peppermint candies to anchor a scented votive candle...a pretty and easy way to add holiday cheer.

Spinach Feta Puffs

Molly Ebert
Decatur, IN

An oldie but goodie! These puffs make a great appetizer and are wonderful alongside a steamy bowl of soup. I must admit I've been known to make a meal of them!

10-oz. pkg. frozen chopped spinach, thawed and well drained
3/4 to 1 c. crumbled feta cheese
1/2 c. onion, finely chopped
2 T. fresh parsley, chopped

1/2 t. pepper
Optional: 1/8 t. cayenne pepper
3 eggs, divided
1 T. water
17-oz. pkg. frozen puff pastry, thawed

In a bowl, mix together spinach, feta cheese, onion, parsley, seasonings and 2 beaten eggs. In a separate bowl, whisk together remaining egg and water; set aside. Unfold pastry sheets on a lightly floured surface. Roll each sheet into a 12-inch square. Cut each pastry sheet into sixteen 3-inch squares with a pizza cutter. Place one tablespoon spinach mixture in the center of each square. Fold squares over filling to form triangles. Brush edges with egg mixture; crimp edges with a fork to seal. Place on a lightly greased baking sheet. Brush tops with remaining egg mixture. Bake at 400 degrees for 20 minutes, or until golden. Serve warm or at room temperature. Makes 16 puffs.

Look for foil stars at office supply stores... you can get hundreds of stickers for next to nothing They're perfect to stick on purchased glass votive holders. In minutes, you can have gold-star gifts for teachers, neighbors or hand them out as favors at holiday parties!

Tam's Tomato-Basil Squares

Tami Seastrom
Bolingbrook, IL

Guests will be wowed by this appetizer pizza!

2 t. all-purpose flour
11-oz. tube refrigerated pizza
   crust
2 c. shredded mozzarella cheese,
   divided
1 clove garlic, pressed

2 to 4 plum tomatoes, thinly
   sliced
1/4 c. shredded Parmesan cheese
2 T. fresh basil, snipped,
   or 2 t. dried basil
2/3 c. mayonnaise

Sprinkle flour on a baking sheet. Spread crust on baking sheet. Sprinkle crust with one cup mozzarella cheese and garlic. Arrange tomato slices in a thin layer over cheese; set aside. In a bowl, combine remaining mozzarella cheese and other ingredients. Mix well; spread evenly over tomatoes. Bake at 375 degrees for 15 to 20 minutes, until bubbly and golden. Cut into squares. Makes 8 to 12 servings.

Giftwrap designed by children sends extra love with gifts
from the kitchen to grandparents, aunts and uncles.
Use recent drawings as the wrapping paper, or make
extra-large photocopies. Tie on a rick-rack bow.

Sweet-and-Sour Glazed Party Bites
Susie Backus
Gooseberry Patch

I remember my mom making these for every special celebration. Meatballs or cocktail sausages...your choice. They're both tasty!

1 c. pineapple juice
1/2 c. vinegar
3 T. all-purpose flour
2 t. dry mustard

1 c. brown sugar, packed
16-oz. pkg. frozen meatballs, thawed, or 14-oz. pkg. mini smoked sausages

In a large saucepan, mix all ingredients except meatballs or sausages. Bring to a boil over medium heat. Cook, stirring frequently, until thickened. Add meatballs or sausages; stir to coat and simmer until heated through. May be kept warm in a slow cooker on low setting. Serves 8.

Ribbon-covered buttons are so pretty when used to decorate packages, and covered-button kits can easily be found at craft or fabric stores. Simply wrap each button top with ribbon, then snap on the back. It's so easy!

OPEN HOUSE...
You're Invited!

Christmas Crickets

LaShelle Brown
Mulvane, KS

This yummy party food is always requested around the holidays. I think they are called "crickets" because they sing a little when they cook.

1 lb. turkey bacon
8-oz. can whole water chestnuts, drained
1 c. catsup

1/2 c. brown sugar, packed
2 t. dried, minced onion
2 T. water

Cut bacon slices in half. Wrap each water chestnut with a piece of bacon; fasten with a wooden toothpick and set aside. Combine remaining ingredients in a small saucepan. Simmer over medium-low heat until brown sugar dissolves and onion puffs up. Dip chestnuts in sauce; place on a broiler pan. Broil until bubbly and bacon is crisp. Keep warm on a hot plate or in a warm skillet. Serves 6 to 8.

Bacon-Wrapped Smokies

Nancy Bosse
Wamego, KS

My friend Vickie shared this recipe with me. I've taken it to many parties, and people literally dive after the plate. There are never any leftovers, and they are so easy! We usually double the recipe.

1 lb. bacon
14-oz. pkg. mini smoked sausages

1 c. brown sugar, packed

Cut bacon slices in half. Wrap each sausage with a piece of bacon; fasten with a wooden toothpick. Arrange sausages on aluminum foil-lined baking sheets. Sprinkle brown sugar generously over sausages. Bake at 350 degrees for 45 to 60 minutes, until bubbly and bacon is crisp. Serves 16.

Make some amusing party picks in no time! Attach tiny, shiny ornament balls to long toothpicks with craft glue.

Batter-Fried Chicken Wings

Renee Shock
Beaver Dams, NY

*I love this recipe...mmm good! My sister Sandi gave it to me years ago,
and everyone likes this crispy treat. I hope you enjoy it too.*

1 c. all-purpose flour
1 t. baking powder
1/2 t. salt
1 egg, beaten

1 c. milk
oil for deep frying
24 chicken wings

In a bowl, stir together all ingredients except oil and chicken wings;
set aside. In a large deep saucepan, heat several inches of oil to
360 degrees over medium-high heat. Dip wings in batter. Fry wings,
a few at a time, for 5 minutes, or until golden and cooked through.
Drain on paper towels. Makes 2 dozen.

Just for fun, slip party invitations inside woolly mittens,
then deliver to family & friends.

3-Pepper Chicken Bites

Amy Bradsher
Roxboro, NC

This is such a fun appetizer for a party! Sweet with a kick, it can be tossed together quickly and ready for the oven when your guests arrive. How can you go wrong with bacon?

1/2 lb. bacon
1 lb. boneless, skinless chicken breasts, cut into one-inch cubes

2/3 c. brown sugar, packed
1 t. cayenne pepper
1 t. chili powder
1/8 t. pepper

Cut bacon slices in thirds. Wrap each piece of chicken with a strip of bacon and fasten with a wooden toothpick; set aside. Mix together remaining ingredients in a small bowl. Dredge each piece in brown sugar mixture. Place on a wire rack on an aluminum foil-lined baking sheet. Bake at 350 degrees for 30 to 35 minutes, until chicken juices run clear and bacon is crisp. Makes 2 to 2-1/2 dozen.

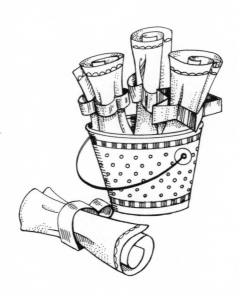

Shop yard sales and thrift stores for all kinds of cookie cutters... they make terrific napkin rings, ornaments and package tie-ons.

Amy's Caramelized Onion Tartlets

Eleanor Dionne
Beverly, MA

Amy is my son Eric's girlfriend, and we have known her since she was a little girl. This is one of her special recipes. She makes these for parties, and everyone eats lots of them...you can't stop at just one or two!

1/2 c. plus 2 T. butter, divided	1 T. beef bouillon granules
2 sweet onions, chopped	1 c. shredded Swiss cheese
1/4 c. sugar	8 14-inch by 9-inch sheets
3/4 c. hot water	phyllo dough, thawed

In a large skillet, melt 2 tablespoons butter over medium heat. Add onions; sprinkle with sugar. Cook for 15 to 20 minutes, until onions are golden, stirring frequently. Stir in water and bouillon; bring to a boil. Reduce heat; simmer, uncovered, for 5 to 7 minutes, until liquid has evaporated. Remove from heat; stir in cheese and set aside. Melt remaining butter. Place one sheet of phyllo dough on a work surface; brush evenly with butter. Top with a second sheet of phyllo dough; brush with butter and cut into 12 squares. Keep remaining dough covered with plastic wrap and a damp tea towel to prevent drying out. Repeat 3 times, making 48 squares. Press one dough square into a greased mini muffin cup. Top with another square, placing corners off-center. Spoon one tablespoon onion mixture into cup. Repeat with remaining dough squares and onion mixture. Bake at 375 degrees for 10 to 15 minutes, until golden. Serve warm. Makes 2 dozen.

From Thanksgiving to New Year's Day, set out a guest book whenever friends come to visit! Ask everyone young and old to sign...it's sure to become a treasured memento.

OPEN HOUSE...
You're Invited!

Cheddar Ha'Pennies

Vickie

*A terrific little treat that goes very well with holiday beverages!
Freeze the logs of dough up to two months, wrapped in plastic wrap,
for pop-in guests. Just thaw slightly, slice and bake.*

8-oz. pkg. shredded sharp
   Cheddar cheese
1 c. all-purpose flour

1/2 c. butter, softened
3 T. onion soup mix

Combine all ingredients in a large bowl; mix well. Knead into a smooth ball; divide dough in half. Form each half into a log, one-inch in diameter. Wrap in wax paper and chill for 2 hours. Slice logs 1/4-inch thick. Arrange on ungreased baking sheets. Bake at 375 degrees for 10 to 12 minutes, watching carefully, until golden but not browned. Makes about 3 dozen.

Christmas is coming, the geese are getting fat,
Please to put a penny in an old man's hat.
If you haven't got a penny, then a ha'penny will do,
If you haven't got a ha'penny, then God bless you!
–Traditional English Carol

Mimi Brasel's Dazzles

Candy Brasel
Grove, OK

My mother-in-law had a passion for making special things for her family. Christmas was her favorite holiday. This is her original recipe passed down through the years, and it's always served at family gatherings. Keep the cheese mixture handy in the refrigerator for a quick party snack!

1-1/2 c. shredded sharp Cheddar
    cheese
1/2 c. mayonnaise
1 c. chopped black olives,
    drained

1/2 c. green onions, thinly sliced
1/2 t. salt
1/8 t. curry powder
1 loaf party rye bread

Mix together all ingredients except bread in a bowl; set aside. Arrange bread slices on a broiler pan; toast on one side. Turn over slices; spread generously with cheese mixture. Broil until cheese melts, watching carefully. Makes about 3 dozen.

Childhood toys add a feel of nostalgia to Christmas displays.
Sailboats, airplanes, teddy bears, dolls or tea sets all bring
back fond memories. Set them on tables, stairs,
cupboard shelves or mantels.

OPEN HOUSE...
You're Invited!

Homemade Soft Pretzels

Melody Chencharick
Julian, PA

*This fun recipe is a terrific memory maker to do with your children...
kneading the dough is a great job for the kids! The pretzels
can even be shaped into HO-HO's for the holidays.*

1-1/2 c. warm water
1 env. dry active yeast
1 T. sugar
1 t. salt

4 c. all-purpose flour
1 egg, beaten
Garnish: coarse salt

Heat water until very warm, about 110 to 115 degrees. In a large bowl,
dissolve yeast in warm water; add sugar and salt. Blend in flour. On a
lightly floured surface, knead dough until smooth. Roll pieces of dough
into long ropes; form into twists or sticks. Place pretzels on lightly
greased baking sheets. Brush with egg; sprinkle with coarse salt. Bake
at 425 degrees for 12 to 15 minutes, until lightly golden. Makes 8 to
10 pretzels.

The golden glow of
candlelight adds a magic
touch to any gathering.
For all the charm of real
flames, use battery-operated
candles and tealights...there's
no need to worry about little
ones or pets touching them.

115

Creamy Spinach & Onion Dip

Janis Greene
Brandon, FL

This is my favorite dip...it's a big hit at every party!

3 8-oz. pkgs. cream cheese, softened
2 c. shredded Italian-blend cheese
10-oz. pkg. frozen chopped spinach, thawed and well drained
10-oz. pkg. frozen chopped onions, thawed and well drained
3-oz. pkg. bacon crumbles
crackers or chips

In a large bowl, combine all ingredients except chips or crackers; mix well. Spoon mixture into a lightly greased 2-quart casserole dish. Bake, uncovered, at 350 degrees for 30 minutes, or until hot and bubbly. Serve warm with chips or crackers. Makes 20 servings.

Winter's snow can dust even your mailbox with magic. Put a smile on your postman's face and turn yours into a gingerbread house, with sprigs of evergreen, tiny windows, even a roof of shingles. Don't forget to leave a treat inside, too!

Italian Chicken Spread

Patrice Lindsey
Lockport, IL

This makes a yummy appetizer or luncheon spread.

13-oz. can chicken, drained,
   or 1-1/2 c. cooked chicken
1/3 c. mayonnaise
1/3 c. Italian salad dressing

1/3 c. grated Parmesan cheese
1 t. Italian seasoning
crackers or lightly toasted Italian
   bread slices

Place chicken in a bowl; flake or shred finely. Add remaining ingredients except crackers or bread; stir well to combine. Cover and chill for 2 to 3 hours to allow flavors to blend. Serve at room temperature, or bake at 350 degrees until hot and bubbly. Serve with crackers or bread. Makes 2-1/2 cups.

Create super party favors in a jiffy. Dip clear ornaments into bright white latex paint and dust with mica snow. Slip the ornament hanger in place, then hang to dry. Pile in a bowl for guests to take home.

Party Shrimp Marinade

Linda Stone
Algood, TN

This delicious shrimp is always welcome at get-togethers!

2 c. onions, sliced
8 bay leaves
1-1/2 c. white vinegar
2-1/2 t. celery seed
1-1/2 t. salt

1 t. hot pepper sauce
2-1/2 lbs. medium to large
   shrimp, cleaned and cooked
party rye bread

In a large bowl, mix all ingredients except shrimp and bread. Add shrimp; stir. Cover and refrigerate for at least 24 hours. Drain; discard bay leaves. Serve with party rye bread. Serves 10, depending on size of shrimp.

Curry Dip for Shrimp Cocktail

Penni Nicholson
Quebec, Canada

My daughter Karen loves shrimp but not the marinara cocktail sauce.
So I created this yummy curry dip to go along with the shrimp,
and it was an instant hit!

1 c. mayonnaise
2 t. onion, grated
1 t. prepared horseradish

1 t. curry powder
1 t. garlic salt
1/2 t. dried tarragon

Combine all ingredients; blend well. Cover and chill before serving. Makes about one cup.

Bring a bit of retro to the
holiday kitchen...tie on
a vintage Christmas apron!

OPEN HOUSE...
You're Invited!

Favorite Salmon Ball

Loury Johnson
Colorado Springs, CO

When I was a kid, Mom would make nearly 20 of these tasty salmon balls every holiday season for us to to enjoy and to give as gifts. This recipe is easily doubled or tripled.

2 6-oz. cans salmon, drained
   and flaked
8-oz. pkg. cream cheese,
   softened
2 T. smoke-flavored cooking
   sauce

1 c. finely chopped pecans or
   walnuts, or 1/2 c. dried
   parsley
savory crackers

In a bowl, mix together salmon and cream cheese. Add sauce; stir very well. Cover and chill for 30 minutes. Form into one large or 2 smaller balls. Sprinkle nuts or parsley on a large piece of wax paper. Gently set ball on coating; roll and pat until well coated. Place on a serving plate; cover and chill for at least one hour before serving. Serve with crackers. Makes one large ball or 2 small balls.

Irresistible Crab Dip

Donna Guthrie
North Benton, OH

This dip is excellent...my husband and I can eat the whole thing by ourselves! My daughter received this recipe from her mother-in-law and shared it with me.

8-oz. pkg. cream cheese,
   softened
2 T. milk
1/2 c. mayonnaise
1 onion, diced

1 t. prepared horseradish,
   or more to taste
6-oz. can crabmeat, drained
   and flaked
crackers

In a bowl, blend together cream cheese and milk. Add mayonnaise; beat with an electric mixer on low speed until fluffy. Fold in remaining ingredients except crackers; spoon into an ungreased 9" pie plate. Bake, uncovered, at 325 degrees for 30 to 35 minutes, until golden on top. Serve warm with crackers. Makes 1-1/2 cups.

Sweet Onion Shrimp Spread

Dana Cunningham
Lafayette, LA

Mmm...two of my favorite flavors in one yummy spread!

8-oz. pkg. cream cheese,
   softened
1/2 c. mayonnaise
1-1/2 t. lemon juice
1-1/2 t. Worcestershire sauce
1/2 c. celery, minced

1/2 c. sweet onion, minced
6-oz. can tiny shrimp, drained,
   or 1/2 c. cooked shrimp,
   chopped
crackers

In a bowl, combine cream cheese, mayonnaise, lemon juice and Worcestershire sauce; stir until smooth. Add celery, onion and shrimp; mix until well blended. Cover and chill for at least one hour. Serve with crackers. Makes 2 cups.

Hosting a game-day get-together? Show your spirit...build a snowman and dress him up in a hometown football jersey.
Go team!

OPEN HOUSE...
You're Invited!

Scrumptious Stuffed Mushrooms

Lori Peterson
Effingham, KS

I love to make stuffed mushrooms for parties. I love to eat them too!
The stuffing makes these perfect for Thanksgiving and Christmas.

6-oz. pkg. chicken-flavored
   stuffing mix
1-1/2 c. hot water
2 lbs. fresh mushrooms, stems
   removed and reserved
2 T. butter

2 t. garlic, minced
10-oz. pkg. frozen chopped
   spinach, thawed and drained
1 c. shredded mozzarella cheese
1 c. grated Parmesan cheese

In a bowl, toss together stuffing and water; set aside. Chop mushroom stems. Melt butter in a skillet over medium heat; sauté mushroom stems and garlic until tender. Add stem mixture and remaining ingredients to stuffing mixture; mix well. Spoon mixture into mushroom caps; place in an ungreased shallow 13"x9" baking pan. Bake, uncovered, at 400 degrees for 20 minutes, or until heated through and tender. Serve warm. Makes 15 to 20 servings.

If you have a grapevine wreath that's become a bit tattered,
spray paint it all white, then sprinkle on fine white glitter
for icy sparkle. The textures will pop out and a whole
new wreath will emerge.

Beef in Wine on Potato Rolls

Pat Sohns
Burlington, WI

This is a delicious do-ahead recipe that my mother clipped from a newspaper back in the 70s. My sister likes to make it just the way it's written, but I double the sauce ingredients because we like lots of sauce on our sandwiches. Beef in Wine may be made several days in advance and refrigerated...the flavor improves as the beef marinates in the sauce. It also freezes well.

5-lb. top round or boneless
    rolled beef roast
1/2 c. butter, divided
3/4 c. light dry sherry or
    beef broth
3/4 lb. sweet onion, sliced
2 T. Worcestershire sauce

juice of 1/2 lemon
1/2 t. salt
8-oz. can sliced mushrooms,
    drained
3 cubes beef bouillon
1-1/2 c. hot water
16 potato rolls, split

In a large skillet over medium-high heat, brown roast on all sides in 1/4 cup butter. Transfer roast to a roasting pan. Bake, uncovered, at 325 degrees for 2 hours. Pour sherry or broth over roast; bake one additional hour. Remove roast from pan to a platter, reserving pan juices. In same skillet, melt remaining butter. Sauté onion until golden; add Worcestershire sauce, lemon juice, salt, mushrooms and juices from roast. Dissolve bouillon cubes in hot water; add to mixture in skillet. Simmer for 5 minutes. Slice roast and return to roasting pan; pour onion mixture over beef. Bake, covered at 325 degrees for an additional 45 minutes. Serve beef on rolls. Makes 16 servings.

Mini sandwiches are fun for parties...everyone can take just what they want! Instead of full-size buns, set out mini brown & serve rolls, bagels or or other petite breads, arranged on a tiered cake stand.

OPEN HOUSE...
You're Invited!

Taverns

Joan Cady
Saint Michael, MN

As far back as I can remember, these sandwiches have been a staple for family gatherings large and small. My mother had a pressure cooker that she used for making three things: popcorn, chili and Taverns. They are almost always served on homemade buns.

2 lbs. ground beef round
2 to 3 green onions, chopped
1/2 t. salt
1/4 t. pepper
10-3/4 oz. can chicken gumbo
    soup, partially drained

10-3/4 oz. can tomato soup
2 T. mustard
1 T. catsup
12 sandwich buns, split
12 slices American cheese

In a skillet over medium heat, brown beef with onions, salt and pepper; drain. Reduce heat to low; stir in remaining ingredients except buns and cheese. Simmer until heated through; the longer it simmers, the better the flavor. Serve spooned on buns and topped with a slice of American cheese. Makes one dozen sandwiches.

If there's a historic village nearby, bundle up the kids and go for a visit. Many times the village will have special holiday programs...strolling carolers in vintage costumes, sleigh rides or special recitals in the town hall. You might even find someone roasting chestnuts!

Jennifer's Holiday Snack Mix

Jennifer Armenia
Cohoes, NY

I come from a long line of snackers. Family gatherings can get quite contentious as we vie for the best savory snack mix! I might be biased, but I am partial to mine, which I developed over the past 20 years. It's not a low-cal, low-carb treat, so I only make it between Thanksgiving and New Year's Eve, but it's worth it!

1/2 c. plus 2 T. butter
1/4 c. Worcestershire sauce
8 t. lemon juice
1 t. garlic powder
1 t. onion powder
6 c. bite-size crispy corn and rice cereal squares
2 c. bite-size crispy wheat cereal squares
2 c. bite-size crispy rice cereal squares

2 c. bite-size crispy corn cereal squares
1-1/2 c. doughnut-shaped oat cereal
1-1/2 c. pretzel sticks, broken
1-1/2 c. mini round buttery crackers or plain fish-shaped crackers
1-1/2 c. dry-roasted cashews or mixed nuts

In a small microwave-safe bowl, combine butter, Worcestershire sauce, lemon juice and seasonings. Microwave on high until butter is melted. Stir well; set aside. In a large roasting pan, combine remaining ingredients. Stir well to mix. Drizzle butter mixture over cereal mixture, stirring to coat cereal as evenly as possible. Bake, uncovered, at 250 degrees for 45 minutes, stirring every 15 minutes. Serve warm. Store in an airtight container. Makes about 18 cups.

Celebrate the New Year early with little ones who won't make it 'til midnight. Get out those noisemakers and toast with sparkling juice!

OPEN HOUSE...
You're Invited!

Hawaiian Snack Mix

June Sabatinos
Billings, MT

I found this recipe in a Denver newspaper years ago and have modified it over the years. The ginger gives it a wonderful flavor...my family loves it!

3 T. butter
3 T. brown sugar, packed
3 T. honey
2 t. ground ginger
1/2 t. salt

6-oz. jar macadamia nuts
   or mixed nuts
2 c. mini pretzel twists
3/4 c. dried pineapple, papaya
   and mango mix, diced

In a large skillet, melt butter over medium heat. Stir in brown sugar, honey, ginger and salt. Cook about 2 minutes, stirring constantly, until bubbly. Add remaining ingredients. Cook about one minute, stirring constantly, until all ingredients are coated. Spread mixture in a thin layer in an aluminum foil-lined 15"x10" jelly-roll pan. Bake at 350 degrees for 10 to 12 minutes, stirring occasionally, until bubbly and lightly golden. Spread mixture in a thin layer on an unlined jelly-roll pan. Cool completely; store in an airtight container. Makes 8 servings.

Wrap up treats in holiday napkins, tie with a bow and add a tag stamped, "Thanks for all you do!" Make up a batch to hand out to the mail carrier, the babysitter, the dog groomer, the bus driver and all those other oh-so-helpful folks we just don't remember to thank as often as we should.

Sue's Holiday Mocha Punch

Sue Neely
Greenville, IL

*This is a creamy chocolate punch that everyone loves and
my kids always ask for it during the holidays. I usually make
a double batch...you'll want more than one cup!*

1-1/2 qts. water
1/2 c. sugar
1/2 c. chocolate drink mix
1/4 c. instant coffee granules

1/2 gal. vanilla ice cream
1/2 gal. chocolate ice cream
Optional: whipped cream

In a large saucepan over high heat, bring water to a boil; remove from
heat. Add sugar, drink mix and coffee granules; stir until dissolved.
Cover and refrigerate for several hours to overnight. At serving time,
pour mixture into a punch bowl. Add ice creams by spoonfuls, stirring
until partially melted. Garnish with whipped cream, if desired. Makes
about 5 quarts.

Easy Peppermint Eggnog

Janis Greene
Brandon, FL

*I first tasted this eggnog at a church function and loved it. Luckily the
girl who made it is generous about sharing her recipes! Hang mini
candy canes around the edge of the punch bowl just for fun.*

1 qt. eggnog
1/2 gal. peppermint ice cream,
   softened

1 ltr. club soda, chilled
Garnish: peppermint candies,
   crushed

Stir together eggnog, ice cream and club soda in a punch bowl. Sprinkle
with crushed candies; serve immediately. To make in advance, combine
all ingredients except candies; refrigerate up to 2 hours before serving.
Serves 20.

OPEN HOUSE...
You're Invited!

Low-Cal Christmas Punch

*Martha Allen
Jasper, GA*

*This punch smells wonderful as it is simmering on the stovetop.
Cheers to you, and Merry Christmas!*

1 c. boiling water
3/4 c. sugar or 1/2 c. fructose
1/2 t. cinnamon
46-oz. can unsweetened
    pineapple juice, chilled

32-oz. bottle low-calorie
    cranberry juice, chilled
28-oz. bottle diet ginger ale,
    chilled

Combine water, sugar or fructose and cinnamon in a saucepan; bring to
a boil and stir until sugar dissolves. Chill. At serving time, combine
sugar mixture, fruit juices and ginger ale. Serve over ice. Makes about
3-3/4 quarts.

Gather up the neighbor kids and go caroling around the
neighborhood...just for the joy of singing together! Make up
pages with lyrics, or stick to favorites like "Jingle Bells" and
"Deck the Halls" that everybody is sure to know.

Cranberry Tea Punch

Betty Lou Wright
Hendersonville, TN

One of the joys of the Christmas holidays is making and drinking tea punch. This is one of my favorite recipes, and it's great hot or cold. Oh, it smells so good too!

1 gal. water	4 c. cranberry juice
2 c. sugar	4 c. apple juice
6 tea bags	6-oz. can frozen orange juice
3 T. whole cloves	concentrate
3 4-inch cinnamon sticks	1 c. lemon juice
6-oz. pkg. raspberry gelatin mix	

In a large Dutch oven over high heat, bring water and sugar to a boil. Stir until sugar dissolves. Remove from heat; add tea bags and steep for 6 minutes. Discard tea bags. Enclose cloves and cinnamon sticks in a coffee filter, securing with a twist tie; add to tea. Steep an additional 30 minutes. Discard coffee filter and spices. Add dry gelatin mix and remaining ingredients; stir until well mixed. May be served hot or cold. Makes 1-1/2 gallons.

Dress up servings of holiday punch...thread fresh cranberries onto stirring sticks. Quick & easy!

TREE-TRIMMING
Treats

Candy Cane Cookies

Sandra Wetzel
Shawnee, KS

Once when I was little, my family traveled out of state for Christmas. Our sweet neighbor gave us a decorated shoebox full of delicious treats for the trip. These cookies were among them...they will always taste like Christmas to me! Years later, they are our daughter's favorite cookie. Remembering you fondly, dear Doris!

1/2 c. butter
1/2 c. shortening
1 c. powdered sugar
1 egg, beaten
1-1/2 t. almond extract

1 t. vanilla extract
2-1/2 c. all-purpose flour
1 t. salt
few drops red and green
   food coloring

In a bowl, blend together butter, shortening, powdered sugar, egg and extracts. Add flour and salt; mix until smooth. Divide dough in half. Tint one half red, the other half green, or leave one half white. Refrigerate one to 2 hours, until dough is stiff enough to handle. For each cookie, pinch off a rounded teaspoonful of dough from each half; roll into pencil-thin strips, about 4 inches long. Twist strips together and bend one end to form cane. If dough becomes too soft, chill again until firm. Place cookies on ungreased baking sheets. Bake at 375 degrees for about 10 minutes, until lightly golden. Makes about 4 dozen.

Decorate a paper sack with stencils or rubber stamps and fill with cookies. Fold the top over, punch two holes and slide a peppermint stick through for a sweet gift bag.

Peppermint Pinwheels

Brenda Hager
Nancy, KY

I first made this recipe back in 1973 for my young son and daughter at Christmas. They became my son's favorite cookie, requested every Christmas. Now, he's grown with three lovely daughters of his own, and his wife continues the tradition of baking these peppermint cookies each year.

2 c. all-purpose flour
1/2 t. baking powder
1/2 t. salt
3/4 c. butter
3/4 c. sugar

1 egg yolk
1 t. vanilla extract
1/2 t. peppermint extract
few drops red food coloring

Sift together flour, baking powder and salt in a bowl; set aside. In a separate bowl, beat butter and sugar until fluffy; add egg yolk and vanilla. Stir in flour mixture, 1/3 at a time, until a soft dough forms. Divide dough into halves. Add extract to one half; tint pink with food coloring. Leave other half white. Roll each half between 2 sheets of wax paper, to a 16-inch by 10-inch rectangle. Place pink dough on top of white rectangle. Roll up tightly, starting on one long edge and peeling off paper as you roll. Wrap in plastic wrap; chill for several hours. Slice roll 1/4-inch thick. Place slices on ungreased baking sheets. Bake at 350 degrees for 10 minutes, or until firm and lightly golden. Remove to racks to cool completely. Makes 5 dozen.

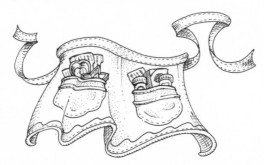

Bundle up a bag of homemade cookies in a holiday apron and tie with a length of rick rack. Tuck the recipe and a cookie cutter or two in the apron pocket. A gift that's sure to please any baker!

Jewel Brooch Cookies

Shirley Condy
Plainview, NY

*When baking for Christmas, I always have to double
this recipe...everyone loves them!*

1 c. plus 2 T. all-purpose flour
1/3 c. sugar
1/2 c. butter, softened

1 egg yolk
1/2 t. vanilla extract
Garnish: candied cherries

Mix flour and sugar in a bowl. Add butter; mix until coarse crumbs
form. Mix with a pastry cutter or your hands until dough holds together.
Roll dough into balls by teaspoonfuls; place on ungreased baking
sheets. Press an indentation in each cookie; top with a cherry. Bake at
350 degrees for 15 minutes, or until golden. Makes 3 dozen.

Mailing cookies is a snap...just follow these tips. Choose firm
cookies like sliced, drop or bar cookies; avoid frosted or
filled ones. Line a sturdy box with plastic bubble wrap and
pack cookies in single layers with wax paper between the layers.
Your cookies will arrive fresh, unbroken and full of love!

TREE-TRIMMING
Treats

Snowdrop Cookies ▶️

Joni Rick
Hemet, CA

I'm always asked for this recipe...it just has Christmas written all over it! This is a wonderful shortcut when you need a quick gift or a treat to share. You can make many variations with this same cookie dough. Use any flavor of cake mix, then add your own touches with different extract flavors and add-ins. Have fun with it!

18-1/2 oz. pkg. yellow or white
    cake mix
2 eggs, beaten
1/3 c. canola oil

zest of 1 orange
1 t. orange extract
1 c. sweetened dried cranberries
1 c. chopped pecans or walnuts

In a large bowl, combine dry cake mix, eggs and oil; beat until well blended. Stir in remaining ingredients. Drop by teaspoonfuls onto lightly greased baking sheets. Bake at 350 degrees for 10 to 12 minutes, until edges are lightly golden. Makes 3 dozen.

Deliver some cookies along with a quart of cold milk and a copy of a favorite holiday story to a friend with little ones...what a nice way for them to enjoy some holiday time together.

Christmas Sugar Cookies

Pat Martin
Riverside, CA

This recipe has been in my family for several generations. It isn't Christmas to us until these cookies are made! It may seem basic, but those who try these cookies say they are the best they've eaten. The key is to bake only until very lightly golden and to decorate with lots of buttercream frosting and colorful sprinkles. Yum!

3 c. all-purpose flour
1 c. sugar
1-1/2 t. baking powder
1/2 t. salt
1 c. butter, softened

1 egg, lightly beaten
3 T. milk
1 t. vanilla extract
Garnish: buttercream frosting,
    candy sprinkles

Mix flour, sugar, baking powder and salt in a large bowl. Cut in butter. Add egg, milk and vanilla; mix well. Divide dough into 2 balls; flatten each to a disc shape and wrap in plastic wrap. Refrigerate for one hour to 2 days, until ready to bake. Roll out each disc 1/8-inch thick on a floured surface. Cut out shapes with cookie cutters; place on ungreased baking sheets. Bake at 400 degrees for 5 to 8 minutes, until very lightly golden; do not overbake. Cool on wire racks. When cooled, frost with stiff buttercream frosting; decorate as desired. When frosting is set, store cookies in airtight containers with wax paper between layers. Makes 6 to 7 dozen.

Slice 'n Bake Sugar Cookie Dough

Give a roll of sugar cookie dough with the decorations included. Yummy chocolate-dipped raisins, bright sparkly sugars and sprinkles make cookie-baking fun. Remember to attach the baking directions!

TREE-TRIMMING
Treats

St. Nick's Old-Fashioned Walnut Balls

Sandy Vance
Sunbury, OH

This recipe goes back as far as 1899, my family knows for sure.

1 c. butter
1/3 c. brown sugar
1 t. vanilla extract
2 c. all-purpose flour

1/2 t. salt
2 c. finely chopped walnuts
Garnish: powdered sugar

In a large bowl, blend butter, sugar and vanilla until fluffy. Sift flour and salt together; add to butter mixture. Mix well; stir in walnuts. Form dough into walnut-sized balls; place on ungreased baking sheets. Bake at 375 degrees for 12 to 15 minutes. Remove from baking sheets with a spatula. While still warm, but cool enough to handle, roll in powdered sugar. Makes 4 dozen.

Orange Coconut Balls

Jill Burton
Gooseberry Patch

When I brought these simple no-bake cookies to the office, everyone loved them! Tuck them into ruffled party cups for a pretty presentation.

12-oz. pkg. vanilla wafers, finely crushed
1 c. powdered sugar
1 c. chopped pecans

6-oz. can frozen orange juice concentrate, thawed
1 c. sweetened flaked coconut

Mix all ingredients except coconut in a large bowl. Form dough into one-inch balls. Roll balls in coconut. Chill until firm. Makes about 3 dozen.

Celebrate a snow day from school with a dessert party. Sweet treats, along with plenty of time for sledding, snowball fights and snowman building, will make for a fun-filled afternoon!

Spiced Gingerbreads ▶

Candice Beaudoin
Nova Scotia, Canada

I grew up making these cookies with my mom all the time. I always got to roll them in the sugar. Now I love making these cookies with my own children, especially at Christmas for Santa Claus. We like to use some colored sugar along with regular white sugar to roll the cookies in. It gives them an extra holiday sparkle!

3/4 c. shortening
1 c. sugar
1 egg, beaten
1/4 c. molasses
2 c. all-purpose flour
1 t. baking soda

1/2 t. salt
1 t. cinnamon
1 t. ground cloves
1 t. ground ginger
Garnish: sugar

In a large bowl, blend together shortening and sugar. Beat in egg and molasses until light and fluffy. In a separate bowl, sift together flour, baking soda, salt and spices; add to shortening mixture and stir well. Form into small balls and roll each in sugar. Place on greased baking sheets, about 2 inches apart. Bake at 325 degrees for 12 to 15 minutes, until golden. Makes 3 dozen.

Dress up simple shortbread cookies with a yummy cinnamon glaze. Combine 1/2 cup cinnamon baking chips with one teaspoon shortening in a microwave-safe bowl. Microwave on high for one minute, stir, then drizzle cookies with glaze.

TREE-TRIMMING
Treats

Layered Mint Brownies

Francie Stutzman
Clinton, OH

When I was young, we always enjoyed these scrumptious brownies with hot chocolate after we went sledding. Yum!

1-1/4 c. plus 6 T. butter, divided
3/4 c. baking cocoa
2 c. sugar
3 eggs, beaten
1 t. vanilla extract
1/2 c. milk
1-1/2 c. all-purpose flour

1/2 t. baking powder
2 c. powdered sugar
1/2 t. mint extract
1 T. water
2 to 3 drops green food coloring
1 c. semi-sweet chocolate chips

Combine 3/4 cup butter, melted, and cocoa in a large bowl; stir until well mixed. Stir in sugar, eggs, vanilla and milk. Add flour and baking powder; mix well and spread in a greased 13"x9" baking pan. Bake at 350 degrees for 30 to 35 minutes; do not overbake. Let cool. Meanwhile, combine powdered sugar, 1/2 cup butter, extract, water and food coloring in a separate bowl. Beat until smooth. Spread over cooled brownies. In a saucepan over very low heat, melt together chocolate chips and remaining butter; stir until smooth. Spread over top. Let cool; cut into squares. Makes one to 1-1/4 dozen.

Warm up a frosty winter's day by inviting friends over for an old-fashioned cookie exchange! It's a nice break from all the holiday hustle & bustle. Keep this get-together simple and have friends bring just a dozen cookies...enough for everyone to sample.

Cranberry-Date Oat Bars

Gloria Linburg
Dover, PA

*I try to make these delicious orange-glazed bars
every year for Christmas. My oldest son Joel loves them!*

12-oz. pkg. fresh cranberries
8-oz. pkg. chopped dates
1 t. vanilla extract
2 c. rolled oats, uncooked
2 c. all-purpose flour

1-1/2 c. brown sugar, packed
1/2 t. baking soda
1/4 t. salt
1 c. butter, melted

Place cranberries and dates in a saucepan over low heat; do not add
any water. Cover and cook, stirring frequently, until cranberries pop and
mixture is pasty, 10 to 20 minutes. Remove from heat; stir in vanilla
and set aside. In a bowl, mix together remaining ingredients except
butter; stir in butter until well blended. Pat half of oat mixture into the
bottom of a lightly greased 13"x9" baking pan. Bake at 350 degrees for
8 minutes; do not overbake. Spread cranberry mixture carefully over
baked layer. Sprinkle remaining oat mixture on top; pat gently. Bake
an additional 20 to 22 minutes. Cool in pan on a wire rack. Drizzle with
Orange Glaze; cut into bars. Makes 2 dozen.

Orange Glaze:

2 c. powdered sugar
1/2 t. vanilla extract

2 to 3 T. orange juice

Mix together all ingredients, adding orange juice to a drizzling
consistency.

If you love fresh cranberries, stock up when they're available
and pop unopened bags in the freezer. You'll be able to add their
fruity tang to cookies, quick breads and sauces year 'round.

TREE-TRIMMING
Treats

Cherry-Almond Butter Bites

Sharon Johnson
Boynton Beach, FL

*My favorite cookie of all time! I created this recipe by adapting
my own ideas to recipes I had come across over the years.
It is a sweet, tender cookie that's good year 'round.*

3/4 c. slivered almonds	1/4 t. salt
1 c. butter, softened	8-oz. jar maraschino cherries,
3/4 c. powdered sugar	drained, 1 T. juice reserved
1 t. vanilla extract	and cherries cut in half
2-1/4 c. all-purpose flour	Garnish: red decorating sugar

In a food processor, finely grind almonds; set aside. In a bowl, mix
butter, powdered sugar and vanilla until well blended. In a separate
bowl, stir together flour, salt and almonds; blend flour mixture into
butter mixture. For each cookie, scoop a tablespoonful of dough; hollow
out the center. Add a cherry half; pinch to seal. Place on parchment
paper-lined baking sheets, one inch apart. Bake at 375 degrees until set
and lightly golden, 8 to 9 minutes. Remove from oven; cool cookies on
baking sheets until cool enough to handle. Dip tops of cookies in
Cherry-Almond Icing; place on a wire rack set over wax paper to allow
icing to cover the entire cookie top. Sprinkle with red sugar. Makes
about 3 dozen.

Cherry-Almond Icing:

2 c. powdered sugar	1 t. almond extract
1 T. reserved maraschino cherry	2 to 3 T. milk
juice	

In a small bowl, stir together powdered sugar, cherry juice and extract.
Thin with enough milk to make a dipping consistency.

For the most beautiful drop cookies and cut-outs, let the
baking sheets cool between batches and grease them
only if the recipe calls for it.

Cathy's Chewy Noels

Cathy Galicia
Pacifica, CA

When we were young, my Grandma Liz always made sweets to bring on Christmas Eve. She passed away two years ago, but luckily she had given me some of her handwritten recipe cards, which I treasure. The original recipe had the option of piping the word "Noel" in green or red icing...but once these cookies cooled, they were usually eaten before she had a chance to decorate them!

2 T. butter	1 t. vanilla extract
5 T. all-purpose flour	1 c. chopped pecans or walnuts
1/8 t. baking soda	1/4 c. powdered sugar
1 c. brown sugar, packed	Optional: red or green icing
2 beaten eggs	

Place butter in an 8"x8" glass baking pan; melt in a 350-degree oven. Tilt to coat bottom and sides of pan; set aside. In a bowl, stir together flour, baking soda and brown sugar. Mix in eggs and vanilla; stir in nuts. Pour batter into pan. Bake at 350 degrees for 20 minutes, or until edges start to become lightly golden. Cool; dust with powdered sugar. Cut into squares. If desired, decorate each square with the word "Noel" piped in icing. Makes one to 1-1/2 dozen.

When you go out on Christmas Eve to attend church services or see the Christmas lights, share a plate of homemade cookies with your local fire house or police station...such a neighborly gesture.

TREE-TRIMMING
Treats

Almond Butter Blossoms

Trysha Mapley
Palmer, AK

These cookies have a wonderful almond flavor, enhanced by the surprise almond in the cookie. They are unique in taste, texture and aroma...a little more refined than peanut butter kisses.

30 milk chocolate drops with
   almonds, unwrapped
1-1/4 c. all-purpose flour
1 t. baking soda
1 c. creamy roasted almond
   butter

1/2 c. butter
1/2 c. light brown sugar, packed
1/2 c. sugar
1 t. vanilla extract
1 egg
Garnish: additional sugar

Arrange chocolate drops on a tray; place in freezer. Whisk together flour and baking soda in a small bowl; set aside. In a large bowl, beat butters with an electric mixer on medium speed until creamy. Add sugars and beat until light and fluffy; beat in vanilla. Add egg; beat until smooth. Add 1/3 of flour mixture and beat on low speed. Gradually add remaining flour; beat until blended. Cover and chill until firm, one hour or more. Roll dough into 1-1/2 inch balls. Roll in sugar to coat; place on parchment paper-lined baking sheets, 2 inches apart. Gently flatten balls very slightly. Bake at 350 degrees for about 16 to 18 minutes, until just golden on bottoms. Remove chocolate drops from freezer; press one into the center of each cookie. Return to oven for one minute. Cool cookies on baking sheets for a few minutes; carefully transfer to wire racks and cool completely. Makes 2-1/2 dozen.

Small packages are a snap to wrap...just cover pint-size plain paint cans from the home center with festive holiday paper. Then fill cans with sweet treats, gift cards and other goodies.

Maple-Pecan Bon-Bons

Tina Hengen
Clarkston, WA

*I often change up the goodies I include in my Christmas treat boxes,
but these candies are always included. They're a family favorite,
and this recipe makes plenty. These freeze very nicely.*

8-oz. pkg. cream cheese,
  softened
1/2 c. butter, softened
6 c. powdered sugar

2 t. maple flavoring
2 lbs. melting chocolate, melted
1 c. pecans or other nuts, finely
  chopped

In a large bowl, beat together cream cheese, butter, sugar and flavoring
until creamy and smooth. Cover and refrigerate about one hour, until
firm. Form into one-inch balls; set aside. Dip candies in melted
chocolate; immediately sprinkle with nuts. Place candies on wax paper
until set. Store in tins lined with wax paper. Makes 5 dozen.

I truly believe that if we keep telling the Christmas story,
singing the Christmas songs, and living the Christmas spirit,
we can bring joy and happiness and peace to this world.

-Norman Vincent Peale

Raspberry Jellies

Teanda Smith
Saint Albans, ME

When I was a little girl, Daddy loved the raspberry jellies in the chocolate gift boxes. Now they aren't often included anymore, so last year I found a recipe for a similar candy, and with a little experimenting, I made the jelly candies myself. On Christmas morning he called me and asked where I'd found these...when I told him I made them, he couldn't believe it! This will be a new tradition for me each year for my daddy.

1-3/4 oz. pkg. powdered
   fruit pectin
3/4 c. water
1/2 t. baking soda
1 c. sugar

1 c. light corn syrup
2-1/8 t. raspberry extract
5 to 8 drops red food coloring
12-oz. pkg. dark chocolate
   chips, melted

In a 2-quart saucepan, mix pectin, water and baking soda; stir until foamy. In a separate 2-quart saucepan, mix sugar and corn syrup. Place both pans over high heat at the same time. Cook both mixtures, stirring constantly, about 4 minutes, until foam in pectin mixture has thinned and sugar mixture is boiling rapidly. Stirring constantly, pour pectin mixture in a slow steady stream into boiling sugar mixture. Continue boiling one minute longer. Remove from heat; stir in extract and food coloring. Immediately pour into a greased 9"x5" loaf pan. Let stand at room temperature for 3 hours to overnight, until candy is cool and firm. Turn out onto wax paper sprinkled with sugar. Cut candy into 3/4-inch squares with a knife dipped into warm water. Dip squares in melted chocolate. Return to wax paper until chocolate hardens. Package in pretty candy boxes or a cookie tin. Makes about 5 dozen.

Delightful vintage holiday cookie tins can often be found at tag sales...just pop in a parchment paper lining and they're ready to fill with goodies for gift giving.

Schoolhouse Peanut Butter Fudge

Sonya Plessinger
Loris, SC

I got this recipe from my Aunt Mary Lee who worked in my elementary school cafeteria years ago. I make it so often I know it by memory. It's easy, with no cooking, and everybody loves it.

1/2 c. margarine, softened
16-oz. pkg. powdered sugar

3/4 c. creamy peanut butter
1 t. vanilla extract

In a bowl, stir together margarine and powdered sugar until creamy. Add peanut butter and vanilla; mix well. Press into an ungreased 9"x9" baking pan; flatten surface. Cut into small squares. Cover and store in a cool dark place. Fudge will dry out somewhat if refrigerated, but will still taste good. Makes 4 dozen pieces.

Cracker Candy

Beckie Apple
Grannis, AR

Cooking has given me lots of enjoyment over the years. I love trying new recipes and also reinventing old recipes. This candy is a reinvented recipe my family really likes.

2/3 c. milk
2 c. sugar
1 T. butter
2 T. creamy peanut butter

1 t. vanilla extract
1-1/2 sleeves round buttery
   crackers, crumbled

Combine milk and sugar in a saucepan over medium heat. Bring to a boil while stirring constantly. Remove from heat. Add butter, peanut butter and vanilla; mix well. Add crumbled crackers and stir well. Drop by tablespoonfuls onto wax paper. Let cool for 30 minutes. Store in an airtight container. Makes 2 dozen pieces.

Tuck candies into ruffled mini muffin cup liners and arrange on a tiered stand...so pretty!

TREE-TRIMMING
Treats

Winnie's Nut & Berry Bark

Darcey Fitrakis
Old Fort, NC

My mom just loves this combination of chocolates and other goodies...
I think you will, too! Pack it in tins or bags for a nice gift.

1 lb. dark melting chocolate
1-1/2 c. sweetened dried
  cranberries

1 c. chopped walnuts
1/4 c. white melting chocolate

Melt dark chocolate in a large saucepan over low heat; stir until smooth.
Add cranberries and walnuts; stir to coat well. Pour onto a wax paper-
lined baking sheet. Melt white chocolate; drizzle over dark chocolate
layer. Let stand until set, refrigerating if necessary. Break up into
serving-size pieces. Store in an airtight container. Makes about
1-1/2 pounds.

Toffee the Easy Way

Julie Perkins
Anderson, IN

I have always loved homemade toffee! Now I can enjoy this
simple and delicious treat year 'round.

1 lb. butter
2 c. sugar
6-oz. pkg. milk chocolate chips,
  melted

Optional: chopped pecans

In a heavy saucepan over medium heat, bring butter and sugar to a boil.
Cook and stir until mixture reaches the hard-crack stage, or 290 to
310 degrees on a candy thermometer. Pour mixture onto a greased
baking sheet. Refrigerate until cooled. Break into pieces; dip into melted
chocolate. If desired, sprinkle with pecans. Place pieces on wax paper;
allow chocolate to harden. Store in an airtight container. Makes about
one pound.

Papa's Fancy Candy Balls

Marty Findley
Boyd, TX

It was a family tradition for my father-in-law, Eugene Milton Findley, to make candy at Christmastime when all of us gathered at the family ranch in the Texas hill country. This recipe was everyone's favorite! Papa is no longer with us, but his memory and this candy are still with us each holiday.

2 16-oz. pkgs. powdered sugar
14-oz. can sweetened condensed
   milk
1/2 c. butter, softened
1 t. vanilla extract
4 c. chopped pecans

14-oz. pkg. sweetened flaked
   coconut
8-oz. bar semi-sweet baking
   chocolate, chopped
1/2 bar paraffin wax, chopped

In a large bowl, combine all ingredients except chocolate and paraffin. Mix well; cover and chill until firm. Roll into balls by teaspoonfuls; chill until firm. In the top of a double boiler, melt chocolate and paraffin. Dip chilled balls in chocolate. Place on wax paper to cool and set. Makes 6 to 8 dozen.

Homemade candy is always a welcome gift! Make the gift
even sweeter...place individual candies in mini paper
muffin cups and arrange in a decorated box.

Homemade Marshmallows

Sharon Demers
Dolores, CO

*When my husband and I were first married, I found out how much
he loves marshmallows and decided to try making them.
Once you've tried these, you'll agree...no others can compare!*

1 to 2 t. oil
4 envs. unflavored gelatin
1-1/2 c. water, divided
1-1/4 c. light corn syrup

3 c. sugar
1/4 t. salt
2 t. vanilla extract
1-1/2 c. powdered sugar

Brush a 13"x9" baking pan lightly with oil. Line with aluminum foil;
lightly brush foil with oil and set aside. In a large bowl, stir gelatin into
3/4 cup water; set aside. Combine corn syrup, sugar, remaining water
and salt in a heavy saucepan. Bring to a boil over high heat; cook until
syrup mixture reaches the soft-boil stage, or 234 to 240 degrees on a
candy thermometer. With the whisk attachment of an electric mixer on
full speed, beat hot syrup mixture slowly into gelatin mixture until very
stiff, about 15 minutes. Beat in vanilla. Pour mixture into pan; smooth
with an oiled spatula. Let stand, uncovered, at room temperature for
10 to 12 hours. Sift powdered sugar onto a cutting board. Turn out
stiffened marshmallow mixture onto cutting board. Cut into squares
with a lightly oiled knife. Dip cut edges of marshmallows into powdered
sugar to prevent sticking. Store in an airtight container. Makes about
3-1/2 dozen.

Pile everyone in the car and head to the local cut-your-own tree
farm. There's almost always creamy cocoa and snacks to share,
and sometimes, even a surprise visit from Santa and Mrs. Claus!

Hungarian Walnut Torte

Mary Fanara-Coleman
Cleveland Heights, OH

This delicious recipe has been handed down for generations...it's our tradition to enjoy a warm just-baked slice spread with butter. I can remember my great-grandmother and grandmother making it, and of course my mother, who taught me how to bake many pastries. I usually make about 15 to 20 tortes at Christmas for gifts.

2-1/4 t. cake yeast, crumbled
5 T. sugar
1 c. warm milk
1 t. salt

4 c. all-purpose flour
1 c. butter, melted and cooled
4 egg yolks, divided
2 t. water

In a large bowl, dissolve yeast and sugar in milk warmed to 80 to 90 degrees. Add salt, flour, butter and egg yolks. Mix very well; form into a ball. Wrap dough in plastic wrap; refrigerate overnight. The next day, divide dough into 2 balls. Roll out one ball to a 12-inch square on a floured surface. Spread half of Nut Filling lightly over dough. Roll up, starting at one edge. Form into a ring, pinching and sealing together the ends with a little water. Place ring in a lightly greased deep 7" round cake pan or on a lightly greased baking sheet. Cover with a tea towel. Repeat with remaining dough and filling to make a second ring. Set in a warm place; cover and let rise until double in size. Just before baking, whisk together remaining egg yolk and water; brush over tops. Bake at 325 degrees for one hour, or until a toothpick tests clean. Cool; slice to serve. Makes 2 tortes; each serves 10 to 12.

Nut Filling:

1/2 c. water
1 c. sugar

1 c. walnuts, finely ground

In a saucepan over medium heat, boil water and sugar, stirring until sugar is dissolved. Remove from heat; stir in walnuts. Let stand until cooled and thickened.

Mom's Best Balish

Deanne Steele
Geneva, OH

*These fruit square pastries are my mom's recipe, and we have made
them together many times over the years. They are a must-have on
our Christmas cookie tray and are irresistible...a family favorite!*

8-oz. pkg. cream cheese,
   softened
1 c. butter, softened
1/2 c. sugar
1/2 t. almond extract

2 eggs, separated
2 c. all-purpose flour
2 12-oz. cans apricot, cherry or
   date pastry filling
Garnish: powdered sugar

In a large bowl, blend cream cheese and butter. Add sugar, extract and
egg yolks; blend until completely mixed. Add flour, one cup at a time;
mix well. Divide dough into 2 balls; flatten each to a disc shape and
wrap in plastic wrap. Chill thoroughly. Remove one disc from
refrigerator; roll out into a rectangle 1/8-inch thick on a well floured
surface. Brush with beaten egg whites. Cut dough into 2-1/2 inch
squares. For each pastry, add one teaspoon filling to the center of a
square. Overlap 2 opposite corners of dough to the center, over the
filling. Bake at 375 degrees for 10 to 15 minutes, until golden, watching
carefully. Sprinkle with powdered sugar; cool. Makes 5 to 6 dozen.

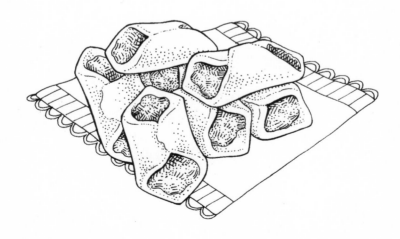

Apple-Walnut Bundt Cake

Madeline Block
Pembroke, MA

Your entire kitchen will smell so nice while this cake is baking!
It's low-fat too, since I use applesauce instead of oil.

3 eggs, beaten
1 c. applesauce
1 T. vanilla extract
3 c. tart apples, peeled, cored
　　and diced
2 c. sugar
3 c. all-purpose flour
1/2 t. baking powder

1 t. baking soda
1 t. salt
1 T. cinnamon
3/4 t. nutmeg
1 c. chopped walnuts
2 T. powdered sugar
2 T. brown sugar, packed

In a large bowl, mix eggs, applesauce and vanilla. Add apples and sugar; mix until well combined. In a separate bowl, combine flour, baking powder, baking soda, salt and spices; add to apple mixture and blend well. Stir in walnuts. Pour batter into a greased and floured Bundt® pan. Bake at 325 degrees for 50 to 60 minutes, until a toothpick inserted near the center tests clean. Cool cake in pan for 10 minutes; turn out onto a wire rack and cool completely. Place cooled cake on a serving plate. Combine powdered sugar and brown sugar; sprinkle over cake. Serves 8 to 10.

For a sparkly centerpiece in a jiffy, arrange shiny ornament balls in a glass apothecary jar. Wind shining silver garland through the ornaments...beautiful!

TREE-TRIMMING
Treats

Snowy-Day Gingerbread

Haley Mounts
Tuttle, OK

My mama began a tradition when I was a child, and it continues to this day...we look forward to it all year long! On the first snowy day of winter, we bake up some gingerbread. There's nothing like a warm piece of gingerbread, straight from the oven, with a cup of coffee while you watch the snow fall!

2-1/3 c. all-purpose flour
1/3 c. sugar
1 c. molasses
3/4 c. hot water
1/2 c. shortening

1 egg
1 t. baking soda
3/4 t. salt
1 t. ground ginger
1 t. cinnamon

Combine all ingredients in a large bowl. Beat with an electric mixer on low speed, scraping bowl occasionally, for 30 seconds. Beat on medium speed, scraping bowl occasionally, for 3 minutes. Pour batter into a 9" deep-dish pie plate sprayed with non-stick vegetable spray. Bake at 325 degrees for about 50 minutes, until a toothpick inserted in the center tests clean. Cut into wedges. Serves 8.

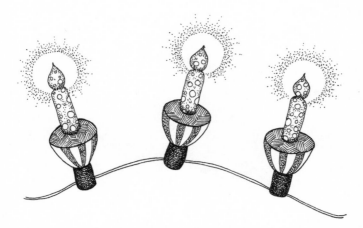

Bundle up the kids and take a ride to see the holiday lights around town. Bring cozy blankets, plump pillows...the kids can even wear their jammies!

151

Old Country Cake

Michele Kearns
Brunswick, OH

My grandmother, Jennie Quass, always made this cake at Christmas. Biting into a piece brings back wonderful memories of childhood Christmases. I love it best fresh from the oven with a tall cold glass of milk. It's even yummy for breakfast if you crumble some pieces in a bowl and pour milk over them.

1 c. milk
1 T. vinegar
1 t. baking soda
6 c. all-purpose flour
1 c. sugar

2 t. salt
1/2 t. cinnamon
1 c. lard or shortening
3/4 c. raisins

Combine milk and vinegar in a large bowl; add baking soda and stir. In a separate bowl, mix together flour, sugar, salt and cinnamon; blend in shortening with fingers until fine crumbs form. Stir flour mixture into milk mixture; stir in raisins. Pat dough out into a large rectangle on an ungreased baking sheet. Bake at 325 degrees for 15 minutes, or until golden. Cut into squares. Makes 8 servings.

Make some old-fashioned surprise balls to unwrap on Christmas Eve. Wrap a strip of crepe paper round & round little toys and candies until the paper forms a ball. Everyone will love unwinding the paper until the surprise is found inside!

Snowball Cake

Sarah Hebert
Cheboygan, MI

This is my new go-to dessert for winter get-togethers. It is easy to make, festive to look at and very tasty.

18-1/4 oz. devil's food cake mix
8-oz. pkg. cream cheese, softened
1 egg
2 T. sugar
3.4-oz. pkg. instant vanilla pudding mix

1/4 c. powdered sugar
1 c. milk
2 c. frozen whipped topping, thawed
7-oz. pkg. flaked coconut

Lightly spray an oven-proof 2-1/2 quart round bowl with non-stick vegetable spray. Prepare cake mix as directed on package; pour batter into prepared bowl. In a separate bowl, beat cream cheese, egg and sugar until well blended; spoon into center of batter. Bake at 350 degrees for one hour and 15 minutes, or until a toothpick inserted in the center tests clean. Cool in bowl 10 minutes. Loosen cake from bowl with a knife; turn out onto a wire rack. Cool cake completely; place on a serving plate. In another bowl, whisk together dry pudding mix, powdered sugar and milk for 2 minutes. Stir in whipped topping. Frost cake with pudding mixture; sprinkle with coconut. Keep refrigerated until serving time. Serves 16.

Make spirits bright by stitching pompoms onto plain winter hats, scarves and mittens. Super-easy to do with just a needle and thread!

Glazed Apple Cream Pie

Jana Jackson
Coweta, OK

My mother has made this pie for years...everyone wants their own pie so they don't have to share! With a cream filling layer topped by apple slices, it's a special treat for many in our hometown.

1/2 c. whipping cream
1/2 c. plus 2 T. milk, divided
1/2 c. sugar
1/4 c. butter
1/8 t. salt
2 T. cornstarch

1 t. vanilla extract
2 9-inch pie crusts
2-1/2 to 3 c. apples, peeled,
  cored and thinly sliced
1 T. all-purpose flour
1/4 t. cinnamon

Combine cream, 1/2 cup milk, sugar, butter and salt in a small saucepan. Cook over medium heat until hot, stirring occasionally. In a small bowl, stir together remaining milk and cornstarch; whisk into cream mixture. Cook, stirring constantly, for 7 minutes, or until thickened. Remove from heat; stir in vanilla. Press a piece of plastic wrap directly over mixture to prevent drying out; set aside. Place one crust in a 9" pie plate; pour mixture into crust and set aside. In a separate bowl, combine apples, flour and cinnamon; toss to coat. Arrange apples over filling. Arrange remaining crust over apples. Crimp edges to seal; cut slits in crust to vent. Bake at 350 degrees for 30 to 40 minutes, until golden. Drizzle hot pie with Glaze. Let cool before slicing. Makes 8 servings.

Glaze:

1/2 c. powdered sugar
1 T. butter, melted

1/4 t. vanilla extract
1 T. milk

Mix together all ingredients, adding enough milk to create a drizzling consistency.

Before adding the top crust to a pie, cut out vents with a mini cookie cutter...little hearts and stars leave the prettiest patterns!

TREE-TRIMMING
Treats

Aunt Ruby's Chess Pie

Deane Osborne
Somerset, KY

When I was growing up, my family would go to Oklahoma for Christmas to visit my grandparents and other family. At Aunt Ruby's house, we watched her make all the Christmas pies and candies...we taste-tested them too! That's one of my favorite memories.

4 eggs, beaten
2 c. sugar
3/4 c. butter

2 T. cornmeal
1 t. vanilla extract
2 9-inch pie crusts, baked

In a large saucepan over medium heat, combine all ingredients except crusts. Cook over medium heat until thickened, stirring constantly. Pour evenly into pie crusts. Bake at 350 degrees for about 10 minutes, or until golden. Cool completely. Makes 2 pies; each makes 8 servings.

Blue-Ribbon Pecan Pie

Gail Kelsey
Phoenix, AZ

This recipe won a blue ribbon at our state fair every time I entered it. It is a family favorite and is always a part of our Christmas dinner.

9-inch pie crust
1/2 c. pecan halves
3 eggs
1 c. dark corn syrup

1 c. sugar
1 t. vanilla extract
1/8 t. salt

Place unbaked crust in a 9" pie plate. Arrange pecans in crust; set aside. In a bowl, beat eggs well. Add remaining ingredients; mix well. Pour mixture over pecans in crust. Bake at 400 degrees for 15 minutes; reduce oven to 325 degrees. Bake an additional 30 minutes, or until center of pie is set. Cool completely. Serves 8.

Place a tasty pie or cake in a basket and deliver to
a busy friend...she'll love it.

Cherries in the Snow

Sharry Murawski
Oak Forest, IL

*Cherries and cream! This is such an easy yet elegant dessert.
I love to take it to potlucks or set it out on a brunch table.*

8-oz. pkg. cream cheese,
  softened
1 c. powdered sugar
8-oz. container frozen whipped
  topping, thawed

14-oz. angel food cake, cut into
  1-inch cubes
2 21-oz. cans cherry pie filling

In a large bowl, beat cream cheese and powdered sugar until smooth.
Fold in whipped topping and cake cubes. Spread mixture evenly in a
13"x9" glass baking pan. Top with pie filling. Cover and refrigerate for
at least 2 hours. Cut into squares. Serves 12 to 15.

Patchwork Christmas stockings are a sweet way to share
a cherished old quilt that's become very worn. Cut simple
stocking shapes from the best portions of the quilt, stitch
together and trim with tea-dyed lace.

Food for the Angels

Carol Irwin
Marysville, MI

*This dessert is delicious! The recipe came from a dear friend 30 years ago. I have a dozen **Gooseberry Patch** cookbooks, and I've never found anything like this in any of them. Enjoy!*

6 egg whites
1-1/2 c. sugar
1 t. vanilla extract
50 round buttery crackers, broken up
1-1/2 c. chopped nuts

1 pt. whipping cream, whipped, or 8-oz. container frozen whipped topping, thawed
2 to 3 c. sweetened flaked coconut

In a deep bowl, beat egg whites with an electric mixer on high speed until stiff peaks form. On low speed, gradually beat in sugar and vanilla. Fold in crackers and nuts with a spoon. Transfer mixture to a greased 13"x9" baking pan. Bake at 350 degrees for 25 minutes. Cool completely. Top with whipped cream or whipped topping; sprinkle generously with coconut. Cover and chill or freeze overnight; cut into bars. May be served either chilled or frozen. Makes 15 servings.

A heavenly host! Round up sweet angel figures to place on a cloud of fluffy angel hair along a mantel.

Bette's Chocolate & Peppermint Roll

Bev Fisher
Mesa, AZ

When I was in grade school, every Christmas my mother made this dessert to take to her women's club meeting. It was the most delicious thing I had ever tasted!

1 c. whipping cream
1 t. vanilla extract
2 T. powdered sugar

9-oz. pkg. plain chocolate wafers
1 c. peppermint candy, coarsely crushed

In a large bowl, beat cream, vanilla and sugar with an electric mixer on high speed until stiff peaks form. Spread a little whipped cream on both sides of each wafer. Stack wafers to form a long roll; place roll on its side on a serving plate. Spread remaining whipped cream over top and sides of roll; sprinkle with crushed candy. Wrap lightly with plastic wrap and freeze for 4 hours to overnight. Just before serving, slice on the diagonal to show stripes of cream and chocolate. Makes 10 to 12 servings.

Take the children to a local ceramic painting shop. They'll love designing and decorating a plate and mug especially for Santa's milk and cookies!

TREE-TRIMMING
Treats

Mint Chocolate Chip Mousse

Krista Marshall
Fort Wayne, IN

I love the flavors of peppermint and chocolate together!
This simple dessert is terrific for busy weeknights,
yet special enough for a holiday treat.

3.9-oz. pkg. instant chocolate
    pudding mix
1-1/2 c. milk
1 t. peppermint extract
16-oz. container frozen whipped
    topping, thawed

1 c. semi-sweet chocolate chips
Garnish: additional whipped
    topping, chocolate syrup

In a bowl, combine dry pudding mix and milk; whisk for 2 minutes.
Chill in refrigerator for 5 minutes, until soft-set. Add extract to whipped
topping and stir well. Fold topping and chocolate chips into pudding.
Cover and chill until serving time. Garnish individual servings with
whipped topping and a drizzle of chocolate syrup. Makes 8 servings.

Top your best homemade desserts with real whipped cream...
it's simple. With an electric mixer on high speed, beat one cup
whipping cream until soft peaks form, then add one tablespoon
powdered sugar and one teaspoon vanilla extract. Continue to
beat until stiff peaks form. Delicious!

New Year's Eve Yule Log

Angela Rose Matz
McElhattan, PA

Every New Year's Eve, my family would gather and share a special meal of steak, lobster tail and this fruit-studded "log" for dessert. Special thanks to my Aunt Teeny for always hosting the party and giving such lasting memories!

2 8-oz. pkgs. cream cheese,
  softened
2 c. sour cream
3/4 c. sugar
2 T. lemon juice
2 drops red food coloring
2-1/2 c. mini marshmallows
16-oz. can fruit cocktail, drained
1/3 c. pecans, coarsely chopped
1/3 c. maraschino cherries,
  drained and coarsely chopped
Garnish: fresh mint, additional
  maraschino cherries

In a large bowl, combine cream cheese, sour cream, sugar and lemon juice. Beat until well blended and fluffy. Stir in food coloring; fold in remaining ingredients except garnish. Spoon mixture into 2 one-pound coffee or vegetable cans. Cover and freeze 8 hours or overnight. To serve, remove from freezer. Let stand 5 minutes. Remove bottoms of cans and push each log out onto a serving plate. Garnish with fresh mint and additional cherries, as desired. Let stand 10 minutes before slicing. Makes 2 logs; each serves 6.

When purchasing a fresh-cut Christmas tree, ask about trimmed-off branches. They're often available at little or no cost and are so handy for adding seasonal color and fresh pine scent to your home.

SLOW-COOKER
Comfort Foods

Spuds & Bacon Breakfast

Mary Lou Thomas
Portland, ME

Every Christmas Eve, I fill up the slow cooker in a jiffy with this recipe's ingredients. In the morning, it's ready for us to enjoy as soon as we've finished opening gifts. Just add a pot of hot cocoa!

16-oz. pkg. frozen potato puffs
1/2 lb. Canadian bacon, diced
2 onions, chopped
1-1/2 c. shredded Cheddar
   cheese

1/4 c. grated Parmesan cheese
6 eggs
1/2 c. milk
2 T. all-purpose flour
salt and pepper to taste

In a lightly greased 5-quart slow cooker, layer 1/3 each of the potato puffs, bacon, onions and cheeses. Repeat layers twice, ending with cheeses. In a bowl, whisk together remaining ingredients; pour over layers in slow cooker. Cover and cook on low setting for 6 to 8 hours. Makes 6 to 8 servings.

Make mini wreaths of rosemary to slip around dinner napkins.
Simply wind fresh rosemary stems into a ring shape, tuck in
the ends and tie on a tiny bow...so festive!

SLOW-COOKER
Comfort Foods

Cheesy Spinach-Ham Strata

Vickie

A satisfying overnight dish that's perfect for a holiday brunch.

1/2 c. butter, softened
10 to 12 slices French bread
16-oz. pkg. frozen spinach,
    thawed and squeezed dry
1/2 lb. cooked ham, diced
2 c. shredded Cheddar cheese

salt and pepper to taste
5 eggs, beaten
10-3/4 oz. can cream of
    mushroom soup
1/2 c. evaporated milk
2 to 3 t. dried, minced onion

Spread butter lightly on both sides of each bread slice; tear bread into cubes. Layer a lightly greased 4-quart slow cooker with half each of the bread cubes, spinach, ham and cheese; season with salt and pepper. Repeat layers, ending with cheese. In a bowl, whisk together remaining ingredients. Pour over layers in slow cooker; cover and chill for one hour to overnight. Cook, covered, on low setting for 3-1/2 to 4-1/2 hours. Makes 6 servings.

Giving a large, hard-to-wrap gift? Just hide it! Wrap up a smaller gift...for example, a bicycle bell for a new bike or one teeny doll for a doll house. Tie on a gift tag hinting at where to look for the large gift...half the work and twice the fun!

Caramel Bread Pudding

April Jacobs
Loveland, CO

Dessert for breakfast on Christmas...we think Santa would approve!

3/4 lb. Hawaiian sweet bread,
   cut into 1-inch cubes
3 eggs, beaten
4 c. milk
1/2 c. sugar

1 t. vanilla extract
1/4 t. salt
Garnish: caramel ice cream
   topping, warmed

Place bread cubes in a lightly greased large slow cooker. In a large bowl, whisk together eggs, milk, sugar, vanilla and salt. Pour over bread cubes; press lightly with a large spoon to moisten bread completely. Cover and refrigerate for 4 hours to overnight. Cook, covered, on low setting for 7 to 8 hours, until a knife inserted in the center tests clean. If pudding is too moist, uncover and cook on low setting for another 20 to 30 minutes. Turn off slow cooker; let stand for 30 minutes. To serve, spoon into individual bowls; drizzle with caramel topping. Serves 10 to 12.

Rich Hot Chocolate

Jamie Johnson
Gooseberry Patch

Equally good on a winter morning or coming home from an afternoon of ice skating! Add a teaspoon of peppermint extract for an extra taste of the season.

3 c. powdered milk
1 c. powdered sugar
3/4 c. baking cocoa
1/2 c. powdered non-dairy
   creamer
1/2 c. chocolate syrup

2 t. vanilla extract
1/4 t. salt
7 c. water
Garnish: marshmallows,
   peppermint candy canes

In a 4-quart slow cooker, combine all ingredients except water and garnish; stir well. Gradually add water, stirring constantly with a whisk. Cover and cook on low setting for 3 to 4 hours, stirring once after 2 hours. At serving time, stir again. Ladle into mugs; top with marshmallows and serve with candy cane stirrers. Serves 12.

Fruity Granola Oatmeal

Tina Wright
Atlanta, GA

I love to serve my kids this hearty oatmeal before they set off for a busy day! Any leftovers can be kept refrigerated for a day or two and reheated before serving.

1-1/4 c. long-cooking oats,
  uncooked
1 c. favorite granola cereal
2 c. milk
1 c. water
1/4 c. apple, peeled, cored
  and cubed

1/4 c. pear, peeled, cored
  and cubed
1 t. cinnamon
1/4 t. salt
1/4 c. chopped walnuts, toasted
Garnish: milk, maple syrup,
  brown sugar

In a lightly greased slow cooker, combine all ingredients except walnuts and garnish; stir gently. Cover and cook on low setting for 7 to 8 hours. Stir in walnuts. Serve oatmeal in bowls, garnished as desired. Makes 6 to 8 servings.

If a white Christmas isn't in the weather forecast, sponge water-soluble acrylic paint over paper doilies for the sweetest snowflake designs on windows. After winter, they easily wipe off with a damp sponge.

Isabela's Special Veggie Soup

Julie Dossantos
Fort Pierce, FL

*I created this recipe for my daughter Isabela when she had the flu.
I wanted to give her yummy warm soup, full of fresh veggies and
lots of feel-better goodness. Serve with crackers or crusty bread.*

2 14-oz. cans chicken broth
14-oz. can low-sodium chicken
  broth
8 redskin potatoes, peeled
  and chopped
3 carrots, peeled and chopped
1/2 sweet onion, chopped
salt and pepper to taste

2 T. dill weed, divided
15-1/2 oz. can diced tomatoes
2 zucchini, chopped
2 yellow squash, chopped
1/2 lb. green beans, trimmed and
  cut into 1-inch pieces
9-oz. pkg. frozen peas
1/2 bunch green onions, chopped

In a large slow cooker, combine broths, potatoes, carrots, sweet onion,
salt, pepper and one tablespoon dill weed. Cover and cook on high
setting for one hour. Stir in remaining dill weed, tomatoes with juice and
remaining ingredients except green onions. Reduce setting to low; cover
and cook for 4 to 6 hours. Stir in green onions in the last 30 minutes.
Serves 6 to 8.

Stack ribbon-tied bundles of sweetly scented candles in
a basket near the front door...a pretty decoration that
doubles as gifts for surprise visitors.

Laura's White Bean Soup

Laura Witham
Anchorage, AK

When I was growing up in Kansas, nothing was more soothing on blustery winter nights than my dad's bean soup. Having deep Southern roots, my family knew how to make beans and greens with the best of 'em! After marrying the man of my dreams and moving to Alaska, I began to experiment with Dad's recipe to create a soup that my husband and I love to eat on cozy Alaskan evenings.

1 lb. dried white beans
8 c. chicken broth
6 to 8 slices turkey bacon,
   chopped
1 white onion, chopped

14-1/2 oz. can diced tomatoes,
   partially drained
1 T. Italian seasoning
1 bay leaf

Rinse beans and drain. Combine beans and remaining ingredients in a large slow cooker. Cover and cook on low setting for 8 hours, or on high setting for 6 hours. Discard bay leaf before serving. Makes 6 to 8 servings.

A snowy winter afternoon is the perfect time to daydream about next year's flower and vegetable gardens. With a tummy-warming soup in the slow cooker, you'll have some extra free time to start leafing through seed and plant catalogs.

My Special Chili

Patricia Lawlor
Ontario, Canada

I know there are a lot of chili recipes out there, but I think I have the best and tastiest! I've used this recipe for years, and it is always requested. Because of the way it is cooked, even though there's a lot of chili powder in it, it has a nice deep flavor yet isn't burn-your-mouth-hot. This chili freezes beautifully as well.

1 T. canola oil
2 yellow onions, diced
1/4 c. chili powder, or to taste
1-1/2 lbs. ground beef
15-oz. can whole tomatoes
2 15-oz. cans tomato sauce

3 15-1/2 oz. cans dark red
   kidney beans, drained
1 t. beef bouillon granules
1/2 t. ground cumin
1 t. kosher salt
1/2 t. pepper

Heat oil in a large skillet over medium heat; add onions and chili powder. Cook and stir until onions are translucent, about 6 minutes. Drain; remove to a plate, reserving drippings in skillet. Add beef to skillet. Cook until browned; drain. Add beef, tomatoes with juice and remaining ingredients to a large slow cooker. Cover and cook on low setting for 8 to 10 hours. Serves 10 to 12.

Give someone an unexpected gift...the school bus driver,
the postal carrier or a new neighbor, or drop off some
pet toys and treats at the animal shelter. It'll make
your day and someone else's too!

LeighAnn's Tortellini Soup

Leona Krivda
Belle Vernon, PA

My niece LeighAnn gave me this recipe. It's very simple to make and so good...it tastes even better the next day! Serve it with Italian bread.

2 T. butter
2 T. garlic, minced
2 48-oz. containers chicken
  broth
10-oz. pkg. frozen chopped
  spinach
2 14-1/2 oz. cans stewed
  tomatoes

salt and pepper to taste
9-oz. pkg. frozen cheese
  tortellini, uncooked
Garnish: shredded Parmesan
  cheese

Add butter and garlic to a large slow cooker on high setting. Stir until butter is melted. Add broth, spinach and tomatoes with juice; lightly chop tomatoes. Season with salt and pepper. Cover and cook on high setting for 2 hours. Shortly before serving time, cook tortellini according to package directions; drain and add to soup. Ladle soup into bowls; sprinkle with Parmesan cheese. Serves 8 to 10.

If you're stringing popcorn garlands on a cozy tree-trimming night, save some freshly popped corn to enjoy as a fun soup topper.

Butternut Crab Chowder

Judy Zechman
Butler, PA

I'm originally from Maryland, so I use only real crabmeat in this delicious chowder! I love this recipe and hope others will also.

1 onion, diced
1/4 c. butter
15-1/2 oz. can petite diced
   tomatoes
2 18.3-oz. containers butternut
   squash soup
1 lb. crabmeat, flaked

15-oz. can shoepeg corn, drained
2 c. chicken broth
1/2 c. sherry or chicken broth
1/2 c. instant rice, uncooked
seafood seasoning, salt and
   pepper to taste

In a skillet over medium heat, sauté onion in butter. Add onion mixture to a slow cooker along with undrained tomatoes and remaining ingredients. Stir well. Cover and cook on low setting for 6 to 8 hours. Makes 6 servings.

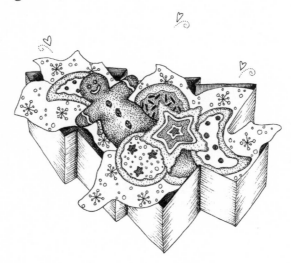

Get together to swap holiday tasks with a friend! If you're a baking whiz, perhaps a friend with elegant handwriting would be happy to address your Christmas cards in exchange for some of your scrumptious cookies. You're sure to think of other ideas.

Feed-a-Cold Chicken Stew

Erin Puleio
Hanover, MA

Who says you can't have chicken stew for breakfast? Whenever I feel a cold coming on at night, I immediately start preparing this stew so that by morning it will be ready. I know it'll make me feel better right away!

1 lb. boneless, skinless chicken
   breasts or thighs, cubed
3 to 4 potatoes, peeled and diced
3 to 4 carrots, peeled and diced

3 to 4 stalks celery, sliced
salt and pepper to taste
2 14-oz. cans chicken broth

Combine chicken and vegetables in a slow cooker. Season to taste with salt and pepper. Stir in broth. Cover and cook on low setting for 7 to 8 hours. Just before serving, add more salt and pepper, as desired. Makes 3 to 4 servings.

Add a little whimsy to an evergreen wreath...tuck in
a little bird's nest and a tiny red bird from a craft store.

Chicken Marbella

Jo Ann

A great combination of flavors...one of my all-time favorite recipes!

1/3 c. white wine or chicken broth
2 T. brown sugar, packed
3 T. red wine vinegar, divided
1-1/2 t. dried oregano
1/4 t. salt
1/4 t. pepper
1/2 c. prunes

1/3 c. green olives
1 T. capers, drained
6 cloves garlic, minced
2-1/2 lbs. chicken legs and thighs, skin removed
1/4 c. fresh parsley, chopped
cooked rice

In a large slow cooker, whisk together wine or broth, brown sugar, 2 tablespoons vinegar and seasonings. Stir in prunes, olives, capers and garlic. Add chicken, pushing down gently into liquid. Cover and cook on low setting for 5 to 6 hours, until chicken is tender and juices run clear when pierced. Stir in parsley and remaining vinegar. Serve over cooked rice. Serves 4.

Angel Chicken

Heidi Butts
Commerce Township, MI

This recipe has received rave reviews...it's wonderful for those December days when you have too much to do!

4 to 6 boneless, skinless chicken breasts
1/4 c. butter, melted
1/2 c. dry white wine or chicken broth
1/2 c. onion & chive cream cheese, softened

10-3/4 oz. can cream of mushroom soup
1-oz. pkg. Italian salad dressing mix
12-oz. pkg. penne pasta, uncooked
Garnish: snipped fresh chives

Place chicken in a slow cooker. Mix remaining ingredients except pasta and garnish; pour over chicken. Cover and cook on low setting for 6 to 8 hours. Cook pasta according to package directions; drain and place in a large serving bowl. Slice chicken and return to slow cooker. Spoon chicken mixture over hot pasta; sprinkle with chives. Serves 4 to 6.

Buttermilk Pork Chops & Mushrooms

Kristin Stone
Little Elm, TX

I tried & tried to get this recipe just right, and I think I finally succeeded! Everyone who has tasted this loves it, especially the thick sauce it makes. It tastes best over hot rice or pasta.

6 to 8 boneless pork chops
salt and pepper to taste
1/4 c. all-purpose flour
1 T. butter
16-oz. pkg. sliced mushrooms
1/2 c. white wine or chicken
   broth

1 T. dried basil
10-3/4 oz. can cream of
   mushroom soup
1 c. buttermilk
Optional: 1/2 t. salt
cooked rice or pasta

Sprinkle pork chops with salt and pepper; dredge in flour. Brown pork chops on both sides in a non-stick skillet; place in a slow cooker sprayed with non-stick vegetable spray. Melt butter in the same skillet and add mushrooms; sauté until tender, about 5 minutes. Add wine or broth to skillet, scraping up any browned bits from bottom of pan. Pour mushroom mixture over pork chops; sprinkle with basil. Cover and cook on high setting for 4 hours. Combine remaining ingredients except rice or pasta in a bowl; mix well and pour over pork chops. Cook for another 30 minutes. Stir to combine before serving. Serve over hot rice or pasta. Makes 6 to 8 servings.

Fill up the slow cooker with a hearty dinner in the morning. After supper, you'll be able to get an early start on a cozy family evening together, watching a favorite holiday movie like *A Christmas Story* or *Miracle on 34th Street*.

Sherried Beef

Kerri Lavoie
Dunbarton, NH

We love to fill up the crock in the morning, go out sledding
and come back to a hearty dinner in the evening!
Delicious made with venison too.

3 lbs. beef round steak cubes
   or sirloin tips
8-oz. pkg. sliced mushrooms
8-oz. can sliced water chestnuts,
   drained

2 10-3/4 oz. cans golden
   mushroom soup
1 c. sherry or beef broth
1.35-oz. pkg. onion soup mix
cooked egg noodles or rice

Mix all ingredients except noodles or rice in a slow cooker; do not
brown beef. Cover and cook on low setting 8 for 10 hours. Stir; serve
over cooked noodles or rice. Makes 6 servings.

"A taste of home" is a thoughtful gift for a friend who has moved
away. Pack up some locally made goodies...jam, salsa, snacks or
cheese. Tuck in some picture postcards, holiday newspaper
clippings and a snapshot of your family holding a sign that says,
"Merry Christmas from back home!" She's sure to love it.

Mom's Smothered Steak

Glyna Ratliff
Amarillo, TX

My mother shared this recipe with me. It's simple and tastes great...real comfort food! Long, slow cooking makes the beef savory and tender.

2 to 3 lbs. beef round steak,
    cut into 4 to 6 pieces
seasoned salt to taste
1 c. all-purpose flour, divided
2 to 4 T. olive oil

salt and pepper to taste
2 10-3/4 oz. cans cream of
    mushroom soup
1/2 to 1 c. milk

Pound beef pieces on both sides with a meat mallet until flattened and tenderized. Sprinkle beef with seasoned salt and dredge in 3/4 cup flour, coating well. Heat oil in a skillet over medium heat. Add beef and brown on both sides; drain. Season with salt and pepper; transfer to a slow cooker. Add remaining flour to drippings in skillet; stir well. Add soup; mix well. If too thick, add milk as needed. Pour gravy over beef. Cover and cook on low setting for 6 to 8 hours. Serves 6 to 8.

Slow-cooker meals are perfect after a day of Christmas shopping. For an easy side, whip up a marinated salad to keep in the fridge... cut up crunchy veggies and toss with zesty Italian salad dressing.

One-Dish Tomato Pork Dinner

Robin Langley
Lake City, SC

One of my family's favorite dinners! Just add a crisp salad and fresh-baked bread, and you are sure to have a wonderful meal.

4-lb. pork tenderloin
15-oz. can tomato sauce
15-oz. can diced tomatoes
15-oz. can stewed tomatoes
6-oz. tomato paste
1 green pepper, sliced

1 yellow onion, diced
2 potatoes, peeled and sliced
8-oz. pkg. baby carrots, sliced
1 c. instant rice, uncooked
salt and pepper to taste

Place tenderloin in a large slow cooker, fat-side up. Pour all tomatoes with their juice over tenderloin. Add vegetables; gently stir in. Cover and cook on low setting for 6 to 8 hours. About 30 minutes before serving time, add rice, stirring into liquid in slow cooker. Cover and cook for another 30 minutes. Slice tenderloin; serve with vegetables and rice from slow cooker. Serves 8.

Few sights are more charming than that of a town covered with new-fallen, clean white snow; and how pretty it is to watch the tiny flakes drift downward through the air.

–Cyril W. Beaumont

SLOW-COOKER
Comfort Foods

Holiday Brown Sugar Ham

Kay Marone
Des Moines, IA

Luscious and so simple to prepare!

7-lb. fully cooked bone-in ham
1 c. brown sugar, packed

2 c. pineapple juice
1/2 c. maple syrup

Place ham in a large slow cooker, flat-side down. Rub brown sugar over all sides of ham; drizzle with juice and syrup. Cover and cook on low setting for 6 to 8 hours. One hour before serving, baste ham with drippings. Transfer ham to a platter; let stand for 15 to 20 minutes before slicing. Serves 10 to 12.

Apple Cider Pork

Lillian Child
Omaha, NE

My family has always loved pork chops with applesauce, so when I had fresh apple cider in the fridge, I decided to try it with a pork roast. The result was absolutely delicious. Leftovers make fabulous sandwiches the next day!

4 to 5-lb. pork roast

4 c. apple cider

Place roast in a large slow cooker; pour cider over roast. Cover and cook on low setting for 8 to 10 hours. Remove roast to a platter; let stand for 20 minutes before slicing. Serves 8.

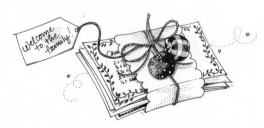

Welcome a new daughter-in-law to the family with this wedding or shower gift. Gather family recipes in a book for her and include all the stories that go along with them.

Hometown Shredded Chicken

Debbie Manning
Wayland, IA

A family favorite! When remodeling my daughter's house, I would toss this in the slow cooker and let it cook while we worked. Serve with baked beans and potato salad or potato chips for an easy meal...yummy!

8 chicken breasts and/or thighs,
   boneless if desired
1.35-oz. pkg. onion soup mix
1/4 t. garlic salt
1/4 c. Italian salad dressing

1/4 c. water
12 hamburger buns, split
Garnish: cheese slices,
   mayonnaise

Remove skin from chicken pieces, if desired. Arrange chicken in a slow cooker; sprinkle with soup mix and garlic salt. Drizzle with salad dressing and water. Cover and cook on low setting for 7 to 8 hours. Remove chicken to a bowl and cool slightly, reserving juices in slow cooker. Shred chicken and return to slow cooker. Serve on hamburger buns, topped with cheese and mayonnaise. Makes 12 sandwiches.

Build a sweet gingerbread house and top it off with chocolate bar doors and shutters. Turn everyone's imagination loose with decorator frostings, assorted candies, even cereal and pretzels! Kids love this...just be sure to have extra candies on hand for nibbling.

Savory French Dip

Amanda Bennett
Rindge, NH

This is a recipe my family just loves. Not only is it fun, but it's so easy to make and tastes delicious!

2-lb. beef top round roast, trimmed
3 c. water
1 c. soy sauce
1 t. dried rosemary
1 t. dried thyme

1 t. garlic powder
3 whole peppercorns
1 bay leaf
4 to 6 bulkie rolls or kaiser rolls
Garnish: Swiss cheese slices

Place roast in a slow cooker. Combine remaining ingredients except rolls and garnish; pour over roast. Cover and cook on low setting for 8 to 9 hours until roast is very tender. Shred roast, reserving drippings in slow cooker. Discard bay leaf. Serve beef on rolls, topped with Swiss cheese. Spoon drippings from slow cooker into small bowls for dipping. Makes 4 to 6 sandwiches.

Fill a large basket with all the groceries for a holiday dinner. Have the kids make a sign saying "Happy Holidays from our family to yours" and deliver the basket to a neighborhood charity. A sure way to remember what Christmas is all about!

Dressing Balls & Gravy

Rashia Redden
Princeton, WV

*Tasty and so easy! The gravy is also tasty on roast turkey or chicken.
Add another can of soup if you'd like to make extra gravy.*

16-oz. pkg. stuffing mix
2 eggs, beaten
2 14-oz. cans chicken broth,
   divided
1 c. celery, chopped
1 c. onion, chopped
1/2 c. butter

1 t. poultry seasoning
1/4 t. pepper
10-3/4 oz. can cream of chicken
   soup
10-3/4 oz. can cream of celery
   soup

In a large bowl, stir together stuffing mix, eggs and one can broth; set aside. In a skillet over medium heat, sauté celery and onion in butter until tender. Sprinkle with seasonings; add to dressing mixture and stir well. Form into large balls; refrigerate for 3 hours to overnight. Place balls in a slow cooker. Combine soups and remaining broth; pour over top. Stir carefully to coat. Cover and cook on low setting for 2 to 3 hours, or on high setting for one hour. Serve dressing balls with gravy from slow cooker. Serves 4 to 6.

Jessica's Cheesy Potatoes

Jessica Kraus
Delaware, OH

*An easy way to make creamy cheesy goodness! Everyone loves
these potatoes, so I usually double the recipe.*

32-oz. pkg. frozen diced
   potatoes, thawed
2 c. shredded Cheddar cheese

10-3/4 oz. can cream of
   mushroom soup
8-oz. container sour cream

Mix all ingredients in a greased large slow cooker. Cover and cook on high setting for 3-1/2 hours, or until hot and bubbly. Serves 8.

SLOW-COOKER
Comfort Foods

Creamed Corn Deluxe

Annette Ingram
Grand Rapids, MI

A side dish worthy of your best holiday roast!

4 c. frozen corn, thawed
1/2 c. red pepper, chopped
1/2 c. milk
1/4 c. butter, melted
salt and pepper to taste

4 slices bacon, crisply cooked,
  crumbled and divided
8-oz. container onion & chive
  cream cheese, softened

In a greased slow cooker, mix all ingredients except cream cheese, reserving half of the bacon for garnish. Cover and cook on high setting for 2 to 2-1/2 hours. Stir in cream cheese; cook 10 minutes longer. Stir well; garnish with reserved bacon. Serves 8.

Zucchini à la Parmesan

Beth Kramer
Port Saint Lucie, FL

When I took this dish to our church potluck, it was a hit!

4 to 6 zucchini, sliced
15-1/2 oz. can diced tomatoes
1 red onion, sliced
1 green pepper, thinly sliced
1/2 t. dried basil

1/2 t. salt
1/2 t. pepper
1 T. butter, sliced
1/4 c. grated Parmesan cheese

In a slow cooker, combine zucchini, tomatoes with juice, onion, green pepper and seasonings. Cover and cook on low setting for 3 hours. Dot with butter; sprinkle with cheese. Cover and cook an additional 1-1/2 hours. Makes 6 servings.

Sending a Christmas card to a dear friend back home?
Tuck in a packet of spiced tea...she can enjoy a hot cup
of tea while reading your latest news.

Sweet Potato-Pineapple Pudding

Kelly Alderson
Erie, PA

My Aunt Mae always used to make an oven-baked version of this dish. This way is much easier, and it frees up the oven to bake the holiday ham.

3 lbs. sweet potatoes, peeled
  and grated
20-oz. can crushed pineapple
12-oz. can evaporated milk
3 eggs, beaten

1 t. cinnamon
1/2 t. nutmeg
1-1/4 c. dark brown sugar,
  packed
6 T. butter, sliced

Combine sweet potatoes and pineapple with juice in a lightly greased slow cooker. In a bowl, whisk together milk, eggs and spices; pour over sweet potato mixture. Sprinkle with brown sugar; dot with butter. Cover and cook on low setting for 7 to 8 hours, gently stirring every 2 hours, until sweet potatoes are tender. Serve warm or at room temperature. Makes 8 servings.

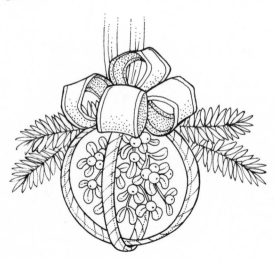

'Tis the season...hang a kissing ball in the doorway!
Make one by wrapping two embroidery hoops in ribbon,
then tie on a sprig of mistletoe.

Bavarian Cabbage & Apples

Melanie Lowe
Dover, DE

*We enjoy this sweet-tart side dish year 'round. It's equally good
with our New Year's Day pork roast and with sausages
on the grill in the summertime.*

1 head red cabbage, coarsely
   sliced
1 c. onion, coarsely chopped
6 Gala apples, quartered
   and cored
2 c. hot water

2/3 c. cider vinegar
6 T. bacon drippings or butter,
   melted
3 T. sugar
2 t. salt

Place cabbage, onion and apples in a greased large slow cooker. Stir
together remaining ingredients in a bowl; pour over cabbage mixture.
Cover and cook on low setting for 8 to 10 hours. Stir well before
serving. Serves 8 to 10.

A pocket calendar for the new year makes a thoughtful gift
for family members near & far. Fill in birthdays, anniversaries
and other important dates. Everyone is sure to appreciate
this gift and use it all year long!

Secret-Ingredient Cocktail Sausages

Tracee Cummins
Amarillo, TX

This recipe came from a local school cookbook I received as a wedding present 26 years ago. I've made these tasty appetizers ever since, for Christmas and other get-togethers where hearty fare was required! The sweet-and-sour flavor is always a hit.

10-oz. jar strawberry preserves
6-oz. jar mustard

2 14-oz. pkgs. mini smoked sausages

Stir together preserves and mustard in a slow cooker. Add sausages; mix gently. Cover and cook on low setting for 4 to 6 hours, or on high setting for one to 2 hours, stirring occasionally. Serve warm. Makes 10 to 12 servings.

Brown Sugar-Bacon Bites

Megan Besch
Omaha, NE

Everyone loves these yummy treats! Perfect for breakfast and brunch...a terrific appetizer for football parties and holidays.

1 lb. bacon, crisply cooked and crumbled
2 14-oz. pkgs. beef mini smoked sausages

1 c. chopped pecans
1 c. brown sugar, packed
1/2 c. butter, diced

Add all ingredients to a lightly greased slow cooker; mix gently. Cover and cook on low setting for 4 to 6 hours. Serves 10 to 12.

Go ahead and unpack the Christmas tableware early in December...even the simplest meal is special when served on holly-trimmed plates!

Sweet-and-Sour Meatballs

Annette Mehl
Bell, FL

A quick & easy recipe my mom gave me several years ago. The ingredients may sound unusual, but these meatballs are always welcome at potlucks and get-togethers.

2 to 2-1/2 lbs. frozen meatballs, thawed
14-1/2 oz. can sauerkraut, drained
12-oz. jar cocktail sauce
14-oz. can whole-berry cranberry sauce
1 c. brown sugar, packed
1-1/2 c. water

Place meatballs in a lightly greased slow cooker. Add remaining ingredients; stir gently to coat. Cover and cook on low setting 2 to 3 hours. Serves 10 to 12.

You've already trimmed the tree and beribboned the mantel... just add a welcoming row of twinkling luminarias along the front walk and your house will be party perfect!

Hot Crab Dip

Sue Ann Sommerfeld
Columbus, OH

This delicious light dip is terrific for anyone who likes to snack along with the crowd, but doesn't want to overindulge.
Serve with crisp low-fat crackers.

1/2 c. milk
1/3 c. favorite salsa
3 8-oz. pkgs. fat-free cream
   cheese, cubed
4-oz. can chopped green chiles

1 lb. imitation crabmeat, drained
   and flaked
1 c. green onions, thinly sliced
assorted crackers or breads

In a greased slow cooker, combine milk and salsa. Gently stir in remaining ingredients except crackers or breads. Cover and cook on low setting for 3 to 4 hours, stirring every 30 minutes. Serve warm with crackers or breads. Serves 15 to 20.

Can't find the perfect gift for Mom, Sis or that extra-special girlfriend? Why not invite her to a leisurely lunch at a favorite restaurant after Christmas, when you'll both have more time to linger over dessert and coffee. She'll enjoy your thoughtfulness!

Warm Artichoke Dip

Carilee Daniels
Newport, MI

Bring some copies of the recipe with you...whenever I make this scrumptious dip for a party, everyone requests it!

14-oz. can artichoke hearts, drained
10-oz. pkg. frozen chopped spinach, thawed and well drained
1/2 c. onion, finely chopped
salt to taste
16-oz. container sour cream

8-oz. pkg. cream cheese, softened
2 1.8-oz. pkgs. vegetable soup mix
2 8-oz. pkgs. shredded mozzarella cheese
1/4 c. grated Parmesan cheese
chips or crackers

Toss together artichokes, spinach and onion in a large bowl. Sprinkle with salt and set aside. In a separate bowl, beat together sour cream and cream cheese with an electric mixer on medium speed. Stir sour cream mixture into artichoke mixture; add remaining ingredients except chips or crackers. Spoon into a slow cooker. Cover and cook on low setting for 1-1/2 to 2 hours, stirring occasionally. Serve with chips or crackers. Makes 20 servings.

No mantel for hanging stockings? Mount Shaker pegs on a wooden board, one for each member of the family!

Curried Party Mix

Joshua Logan
Victoria, TX

Little bags of this anything-but-ordinary snack mix make great take-home favors! Toss in some hot wasabi dried green peas for extra color and spice.

2 c. bite-size crispy rice cereal
1-1/2 c. salted cashews
   or peanuts
5-oz. can chow mein noodles
2 T. sweetened flaked coconut,
   toasted

1/4 c. butter, melted
1 T. soy sauce
1 t. curry powder
1/4 t. ground ginger

Combine cereal, nuts, noodles and coconut in a slow cooker. Mix remaining ingredients in a bowl; drizzle over cereal mixture and toss to coat. Cover and cook on low setting for 3 hours. Uncover; increase to high setting and cook for an additional 15 to 20 minutes. Serve warm, or let cool and store in an airtight container. Makes 6 cups.

Live music makes any gathering extra special for guests. Ask a nearby school to recommend a music student who would enjoy playing Christmas carols on piano, violin or guitar.

SLOW-COOKER
Comfort Foods

Cheddar Cheese Fondue

Theresa Diulus
Seabrook, TX

My Aunt Di and Uncle Joey were my "home away from home" during my college years, and they served fondue on Christmas Eve. I've continued this tradition with our four children, who all look forward to our "Fundue" evening before heading out to look at the holiday lights.

3 c. shredded sharp Cheddar
   cheese
1 T. all-purpose flour
1 c. chicken broth

1 t. Worcestershire sauce
bread slices, apple slices,
   cut-up vegetables

Combine cheese and flour in a bowl; toss to coat and set aside. Pour broth into a saucepan; bring to a boil over medium heat. Reduce heat to low. Stirring constantly, add cheese mixture in handfuls. Stir in Worcestershire sauce; continue stirring until melted and smooth. Transfer to a small slow cooker; keep warm on low setting. Serve with bread slices, apple slices and cut-up vegetables. Serves 8.

Bob's Spicy Sausage Dip

Tonya Sheppard
Galveston, TX

My husband and my brother-in-law Bob have a running contest to see who can create the spiciest, most flavorful dip. Last year we agreed that this was the winner, hands-down!

1-1/4 lbs. ground chorizo pork
   sausage
1/3 c. onion, finely chopped
3 cloves garlic, finely chopped
14-1/2 oz. can fire-roasted diced
   tomatoes

16-oz. pkg. Mexican pasteurized
   process cheese spread, cubed
1/4 c. fresh cilantro, chopped
tortilla chips

In a skillet over medium heat, brown sausage, onion and garlic; drain. Combine sausage mixture, tomatoes with juice and cheese in a slow cooker. Cover and cook on low setting for 3 to 4 hours, stirring after 2 hours, until hot and bubbly. Stir in cilantro just before serving. Keep warm. Serve with tortilla chips. Makes 4 cups.

Caramel Fondue

Michelle Marberry
Valley, AL

*Yum...this sweet dip is perfect party fare! It makes a
delectable ice cream topping too.*

2 14-oz. pkgs. caramels,
  unwrapped
2 14-oz. cans sweetened
  condensed milk

apple and pear slices, banana
  chunks, marshmallows,
  pound cake cubes

Combine caramels and condensed milk in a slow cooker that has been
sprayed with non-stick vegetable spray. Cover and cook on low setting
for 3-1/2 hours, stirring occasionally, or until caramels are melted and
mixture is smooth. Serve with a choice of dippers. Makes 4-1/2 cups.

Fill a big Mason jar with wrapped candies and place it in the
center of the dining table...don't forget to count them first!
Ask everyone to guess how many candies are in the jar,
then send it home with the person whose guess is the closest.

Peanut Cluster Candy

Debbie Driggers
Campbell, TX

A good friend gave me some of this delicious candy...once I tasted it, I knew I had to have the recipe! I knew that it would become a holiday tradition with my family. Now I make this candy every year for Christmas, and everyone is amazed that it's all done in a slow cooker.

2 16-oz. cans cocktail peanuts
2 6-oz. bars white baking
   chocolate, chopped

4-oz. bar sweet German baking
   chocolate, chopped
2 c. dark chocolate chips

Mix together all ingredients in a slow cooker that has been sprayed with non-stick vegetable spray. Cover and cook on low setting for 3 hours. Turn off slow cooker; let stand for 20 minutes. Stir until smooth. Drop by teaspoonfuls onto wax paper; let cool. Store in an airtight container. Makes about 2 dozen.

All wrapped up! A pretty ruby-red glass bowl, filled with candy
and wrapped in clear cellophane, is a very merry way
to tote candy to any get-together. Top it off with
a festive printed ribbon bow.

Christmas Wassail

Susan Buetow
Du Quoin, IL

*I love serving wassail at our annual Christmas open house.
It's always the most-requested beverage...it beats out coffee,
hot cocoa and eggnog every year.*

6 c. brewed tea, sweetened or
    unsweetened
6 c. cranberry juice cocktail
6 c. apple cider or apple juice
3 c. orange juice
1-1/2 c. lemon juice
2 c. sugar

3 cinnamon sticks
1 t. ground cloves
1 t. cinnamon
1 t. allspice
1 orange, sliced
1 apple, cored and sliced
1 lemon, sliced

Combine all ingredients in a large slow cooker. Cover and cook on low
setting for 5 to 6 hours, or on high setting for 2 to 3 hours. Stir before
serving. Makes about 30 servings.

Easy Cinnamon Cider

Hollie Moots
Marysville, OH

*This is a favorite at my annual cookie exchange. It tastes great,
looks so pretty, and no one can ever believe how easy it is!*

1 gal. apple cider

1 c. red cinnamon candies

Pour cider into a large slow cooker; add candies. Cover and cook on
high setting for about 2 hours, stirring after one hour, until cider is hot
and candies are dissolved. Stir before serving. Makes 12 to 16 servings.

Sparkly sticks of rock candy are
sweet for stirring hot beverages.

COMING HOME
for Christmas

Nana's Anise Cookies

Arden Regnier
East Moriches, NY

When I was growing up in Valley Stream, New York, we lived with my grandmother. One of my fondest Christmas memories is of baking with her. I spent many hours in the kitchen with her, but especially loved her holiday anise cookies. She used a recipe handed down by my great-grandmother, who had brought it from the small town of Saint Arnual in Germany back in the 1800s. Nana baked hundreds of these cookies to give to family & friends, neighbors, the postman, the milkman and many others. She stored her cookies in tins at the back of her enclosed wrap-around front porch. My grandmother had ears like a hawk, so there was no sneaking out the door to grab a few cookies! Since the side window was in front of the living room sofa, though, I discovered I could hide behind the sofa, open the window a bit, reach out and open a tin to get some cookies. Nana never did discover how I was getting those cookies, although when I was in my teens, I finally did confess. I still make her anise cookies for the annual Cookie Fest at our church.

Missing Limbs on the Gingerbread Men

Susan Cooper
Kelso, WA

I often bake gingerbread men cookies to hang on our family's Christmas tree. One year, each night as our family gathered to read Scriptures, our son Zach would always choose to sit by the tree. Close to Christmas he couldn't stand it any more and had to 'fess up. He had been secretly nibbling the arms and legs off the cookies! We were shocked that no one had noticed. How funny! And no, he didn't get punished.

COMING HOME
for Christmas

Aunt Nancy's Open House

Debora Montgomery
Pinson, AL

My wonderful Aunt Nancy always loved getting us all together at Christmas, but our families just grew to be too many. So she decided to set aside a day between Thanksgiving and Christmas to host an open house. Her Soup Day was held almost every December for over 25 years in her home in Pinson, Alabama. It was always fun to see what new, whimsical decorations she would have. We all brought cookies to share. There was always hot soup and lots of other goodies! I would make my Swiss spinach dip and white chocolate bars. This is where new favorite recipes were discovered and shared. We made Christmas ornaments and wreaths together, too, and I liked to make a special ornament for her. When we left we always had a variety of cookies and ornaments to take home. We don't get together anymore as often as we would like, but those memories will live on forever. Aunt Nancy still loves Christmas and everything that goes with it! She holds a special place in our hearts, and we so appreciate the fond memories we made with her. How lucky we are to have her in our lives!

Mom's Magical Christmas Eves

Lesley Stoner
Boiling Springs, PA

When I was growing up in Carlisle, Pennsylvania, my mom made
Christmas the most magical time of year, from her famous peanut
butter fudge to vintage Christmas decorations tucked in every corner
of our home to Andy Williams and Ray Conniff records playing on our
old-fashioned turntable! She passed away when I was 19, and now
that I have a family of my own, my big crazy love of Christmas is one
of the best ways I know to stay connected to her. Christmas Eve was
always the most special time. My brothers Todd and Patrick, who were
already grown, would come home the night before Christmas. As we
arrived home from church, the house would begin to fill up with
laughter and the living room floor would become congested with
wrapped presents. I remember Mom wearing a pretty apron over her
best church clothes, whipping up my brothers' favorite homemade
eggnog, putting out fancy little plates of cookies, fudge, cheese and
crackers, and beaming with contentment that all her kids were under
one roof. The sweetest memory of my life is still all of us sitting in that
crowded room around the Christmas tree. My mom has been in heaven
for 16 years. But every year as my dad, brothers and myself along with
our spouses and her six sweet grandchildren still crowd into the house, I
can't help but think about her smiling from heaven that we are all under
one roof for Christmas, still listening to Andy Williams singing carols
and still eating that fabulous peanut butter fudge!

A Christmas Filled with Love

Ruth Thomas
Muncie, IN

The Christmas of 1961, my father was in the US Navy and was on an expedition to Antarctica. With five children in the family, it was important for my mother to be able to receive Christmas money from him. As we got closer to the date, my mother realized that the money would not be available in time for Christmas purchases. I was 11 and the oldest, so she confided her problem in me and requested my help shopping at Woolworth's. Mother had one dollar for each of us for Christmas gifts and she asked me to pick out the gifts! I felt so grand and important as I picked out trucks for my three brothers and a baby doll for my sister. Because of my "adult" responsibility, my mother thought it only fair that I pick out my own gift to make sure I got what I wanted. I selected a "Babes in Toyland" Colorforms set. When we woke Christmas morning, the snow was coming down as my mother turned on the lights of our little tabletop tree. It was fabulous! My brothers and sister loved their gifts and as I opened mine, my mother winked at me...only she and I knew her secret! As the wife of a Navy man, my mother spent many months alone with five children, but she always made it special and fun. My favorite gift that year was the confidence my mother placed in my hands.

Christmas Eve Visitors

Cathy Cole
Saint Augustine, FL

When I was five and my brother Bunker was ten, we were expecting my grandparents (and Santa) for Christmas, but a snowstorm delayed them and they would not be arriving until brunch the next day. We were bundled off to bed to listen for the reindeer hooves, but were both awoken at 2 o'clock in the morning by the sound of laughter and glasses clinking. We learned later that my grandparents were heartbroken that they wouldn't be with us for the Christmas morning melee and decided to risk the drive from Pittsburgh to Detroit in six inches of snow. Bunk and I walked downstairs together, hand-in-hand (the first and last time THAT happened!) and saw my parents and grandparents enjoying a nightcap around the Christmas tree loaded with gifts underneath. We asked if Santa had come and were told yes, of course, that was why they were celebrating! That Christmas, we opened our gifts at 2 in the morning and to this day it's my favorite holiday memory. We were all together for the last time and all the photos taken that morning show a starry black sky!

Santa's Wrapping Paper

Debbie Kennedy
Somers Point, NJ

When my brothers and I were little, we always got to pick out the wrapping paper that Santa would use to wrap our Christmas gifts. One night, we would leave it on the table, and the next morning it would be gone! And on Christmas morning, all our gifts would be wrapped in the paper that Santa got from our house! I did this for my kids when they were little, too, and it was pure amazement on their faces when Santa would come and get the wrapping paper. It's a fun tradition that I hope they will share with their kids as well.

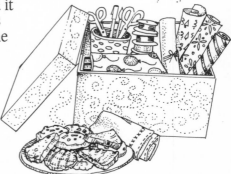

COMING HOME
for Christmas

The Christmas Goodie Box

Susie Wohlwinder
Cynthiana, KY

When I was growing up in Carlisle, Kentucky, in the early 1960s, our family loved Christmas. With five children, I'm sure that Mom and Dad struggled to make our Christmas wonderful. Part of our Christmas was a big banana box full of candy, fruit and nuts. Dad would always go to the local grocer, a good friend of ours, a few days before Christmas and pick up our box. The grocer knew what we liked and he would have it all ready for us. One Christmas, a heavy snow fell and we hadn't gotten our goodie box yet. Our car was snowed in...but never fear! Mom and Dad said that they would take the boys' sled and walk to the store to pick up the goodie box. I was the youngest, so I got to ride the sled as Dad pulled me to town. It was only a few blocks away, but to me it seemed like miles. On the way home, I got to hold the box! My young mind knew that this was a very important job. I had to keep the big box from spilling out all the wonderful things inside. I can still smell the tangerines! Mom and Dad made me feel so special and told me that I had helped make this a happy Christmas. That banana box not only held our goodies, but also a lot of wonderful memories for us!

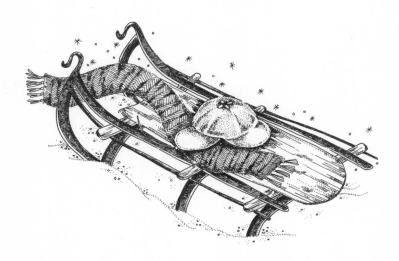

Christmas Angels

Sondra Burnett
British Columbia, Canada

I have four daughters: Bethany Joy, Abigail Joy, Sara Joy and Lydia Joy. Teaching them to be grateful givers was important, especially at Christmastime. I also wanted them to learn to give without thought of return. We began a tradition that has carried over into their adult years now that they have children of their own. It is our own version of Saint Nicholas Day. Early in December, we take a day to make, bake and wrap things for others. We choose about five people we want to bless: perhaps someone with a new baby, someone having a tough time financially or simply someone we are so grateful to have in our lives. After all the gifts are festively packaged, the real fun begins. Everything is loaded into the car and we set out for our destinations. Slowly we drive up the street where our chosen family lives and we park the car. The girls take turns secretly, silently placing the gifts on the doorstep and running away. Over the years, I saw the beautiful giving spirit of our girls grow and blossom. We call ourselves the Christmas Angels.

The Coldest Christmas Eve

Dawn Tenney
Villa Park, IL

On Christmas Eve of 1983, our girls Joy and Sabrina were very young, about three and four years old. We had gone to my parents' home to be with my family. A deep cold spell had set in and it was very cold. My husband began loading our Ford Bronco with the gifts we would take home. He came in to get warm...by now it was ten degrees below zero! He looked at me and said "Houston, we've got a problem." I asked what could be wrong, I thought perhaps he couldn't fit in all the gifts we were taking home. It was worse than that. The back window of the Bronco was stuck in the down position and simply would not go up! After deciding on a game plan, we opted to drive home anyway. We were dressed in holiday clothing so our shoes were not the warmest. I bundled up our girls and put them up front by us. We all bundled up with extra blankets I keep for "just in case" and we turned the car's heater on high. We sang Christmas carols and tried to make the best of it. We dreamed of hot cocoa and cookies. Nothing was said as we went through the toll booths and as a sign flashed the temperature along the roadside, we just tried to avoid seeing how cold it really was. I peeked. It was now 13 degrees below zero! Once we finally arrived home, we all leaped out of the car to go inside and I made a big pot of hot cocoa for us to enjoy with cookies. This memory is a gift, and although they are now all grown up, we still talk of the coldest Christmas Eve.

Going to Cut the Tree

Anita Wilson
Newfoundland, Canada

This is my fondest memory of Christmas past and present. On the 24th of December, our parents, my twelve brothers and sisters and I would get our horses, hook up the sleds and off we went into the woods to cut down our Christmas tree. We would sing carols as we went along, as the snow fell straight from the sky. Then we took the tree home and put it in the shed so the snow would melt off. Into the house we went for hot chocolate and Christmas cookies. By then it was time to put up the tree and we all decorated it before going to bed. This is going back over 45 years ago, and I will always carry those memories with me.

Texas Caroling

Lisa Staib
Broomfield, CO

I grew up in north Texas. When I was a teenager in the 1970s, at Christmastime my church youth group would pile as many people as possible into the beds of two or three pickup trucks. (It was still legal to put 20 people in a truck bed then!) We kept warm with blankets and hot chocolate. We would go to the homes of several of our shut-in elderly members, caroling on their front porches and holding flashlights in place of candles. It might take them awhile to answer the door, but we always gave them hugs, treats and bags of hot chocolate mix. When we got too cold and giggly, we'd pile back into the trucks and drive slowly through the neighborhood, singing Christmas carols. What fun, and a blessing for all!

COMING HOME
for Christmas

Christmas Shopping Downtown

Sandra Smith
Lancaster, CA

Back around 1950, from the time I was ten years old, I began taking my younger brothers Biff and Bill to go Christmas shopping in downtown Cincinnati, Ohio. We'd have maybe a dollar or two in pennies, nickels and dimes and did all of our shopping in the 5 & 10 cent stores. We bought gifts for our parents, grandparents and siblings, and somehow always managed to get a gift for everyone. We'd also visit all the department store Santas to get free peppermint sticks! Back home, we'd sneak things upstairs to wrap our gifts in used, ironed-out giftwrap paper. It's a wonderful memory shared by my brothers.

Santa Said So!

Sandy Coffey
Cincinnati, OH

Oh, what fun it was to grow up in Washington, Pennsylvania! When I was about five years old, we went on our yearly trek to see Santa at the neighborhood 5 & 10 cent store. As my turn came, I hopped up on Santa's knee and told him what toys I wanted...plus the shiny red wagon on display, sitting by his chair! As I got down off his knee I started to pull the wagon down the store aisle when my mom said, "You have to put that back and wait for Santa to come." No, I said, he told me I could have it, so I am taking it now. Needless to say I was not permitted to take the wagon home, but I did get it on Christmas morning. That old red wagon was in our family for years and years to

come, with a new paint job every so often. I tell this story on Christmas Eve to my grandchildren, and to this day I still love little red wagons.

All Hearts Come Home for Christmas

Joan Brochu
Sanford, ME

It was Christmastime of 1985. Our oldest son Chris and his family were stationed in Italy with the US Navy for two years. He was then sent back to the USA and stationed in Orlando, Florida. We were so excited, because that meant our three grandchildren, Joey, Jenett and Jaimie, ages six, three and two, would be coming back and we could see them after two years of them being away. Thinking about this, I got a bright idea! I told my husband, "John, let's go to Florida for Christmas and surprise them!" He agreed that would be great. Then I got another great idea...we would go as Santa and his elf! I was the fat one, so I bought a Santa suit, with cotton fluff for my beard. For John I made a red felt vest, hat and boots with bells, and bought some green tights. Away we went, bag full of toys! When we arrived in Orlando, we stopped at our motel first, changed into our holiday suits and then went to their house. We rang the bell and when they answered I said, "Ho Ho Ho, Merry Christmas!" They were elated...we were all so happy! Our youngest granddaughter was afraid of us and crawled under the couch, but the other two couldn't wait for us to change out of our suits so they could try them on! A very merry Christmas was had by all. Chris was in the Navy for 20 years, including every Persian Gulf conflict, until 1997 when he retired from the Navy. Because of my son being away every Christmas for his Navy years, in his honor I named my business, "All Hearts Come Home for Christmas," because we all know that Christmas just isn't the same without the ones that we love.

Sweet Christmas Tunes

Sena Horn
Payson, UT

One of my earliest Christmas memories began with my mother's well-loved, worn-out collection of classic Christmas records and an old portable hi-fi record player with big detachable speakers. We were living in American Fork, Utah. Each December starting in 1964, Mom would put the speakers in our living room window facing outdoors, surrounded by old rags and cardboard to keep the cold winter air from coming in around them. Each morning as my siblings and I got ready for school, she'd put the Christmas records on to play for the entire neighborhood, much to the delight of the children coming to catch the school bus in front of our home. Her best-loved Christmas albums were by Andy Williams, Perry Como and the Ray Conniff Singers. My own favorite was an RCA Victor album with various artists, from Bing Crosby to Nat King Cole, Dean Martin, Doris Day and Burl Ives. She'd also play the records as we came home in the afternoon, and sometimes at night. This was Mom's way of spreading a little Christmas cheer with us and our neighbors when she had little else to give. Mom continued this tradition for many years, until she and Daddy remodeled the house and replaced this window with a fireplace. As I recall how much I loved this tradition from my childhood, it reminds me that the simplest gesture is oftentimes the most appreciated and most fondly remembered.

A Holiday Kitchen Disaster

Melody Chencharick
Julian, PA

Did you ever have a kitchen disaster? At the time it seems like you'll just die. But now that I'm older and look back, I think to myself, what a great memory! This was around 1993. My sister Charlotte and I were getting together at her house to make Christmas cookies. My son Dustin was four. Take a four-year-old, add flour, sugar and cookie sprinkles and what do you get...a disaster! Everything that went into the cookies was on the floor and then some. All of a sudden we heard a knock at the door. There stood our Aunt Donna and our spotless housekeeper Grandmother. Charlotte wanted to crawl under the table...of all the times for Grandma to visit! Well, we ended up having a very nice visit and Charlotte survived. In 2006 our grandmother passed away. I miss her always and I'm so thankful for that day. Take time to make your own disaster, I mean, a wonderful memory!

COMING HOME
for Christmas

The Christmas Elves

Emily Edwards
Alliance, OH

My favorite Christmas memory is of the "Christmas elves" who would magically find my brother Matt and me every year, even though we moved a lot as we were growing up. The Christmas stockings were faithfully hung by Christmas Eve and we could barely contain our excitement, much less sleep! We should have known Mom was our Christmas elf, making sure our stockings were filled with delightful little gifts and candies, each to our special liking. To me, the stockings were the best part of Christmas. I have carried on our tradition in our family and to me, it remains the most treasured part of the holiday.

First Christmas with Our New Son

Dorothy Beecher
Glens Falls, NY

Our first baby was born in December in the early 70s. My husband and I spent our first Christmas Eve at home with just the three of us. We thought we'd be able to just order a pizza, but back then nothing was open that night. My husband drove around until he found a convenience store open late on Christmas Eve. We ended up having bologna sandwiches and chips for our first Christmas Eve meal together. The next Christmas Eve we decided we wanted to spend it with family, so we invited both of our families to come eat with us if they didn't have other plans. We didn't want anyone to be alone on Christmas Eve! We started this tradition on Christmas Eve of 1975 and have been lucky enough to continue it every year since then.

Midnight Mass With Dad

Sheila Craig Peregrin
Lancaster, PA

Lititz, Pennsylvania, was a wonderful place to grow up, and one of my strongest Christmas memories happened 45 years ago. I was the oldest of four children. Each Christmas Eve my parents would host an open house for family & friends. The "gang" (with their children and later their grandchildren) would stop by our house for a lovely buffet on their way to or from their various church services around town. Everyone would leave by about 11 o'clock so my dad could go over to the midnight mass at our parish church, Saint James Roman Catholic Church, where he was a tenor in the small choir as well as the cantor. The Christmas Eve after I turned 12, Mom stayed home with my brothers and sister and Dad took me to midnight mass with him for the first time. We walked the several blocks together to the church. I was deeply moved by the magnificent service, wonderful music and the beautiful little church which had been festively decorated with greens and flowers, bows and candlelight! When mass was over and we started to walk home, we found that while we were inside, it had turned into a beautiful white Christmas outside! Dad and I walked all the way home singing Christmas carols. As we passed the historic Moravian Church Square, listening to the Christmas music and watching the snow gently fall, I remember thinking that this walk home with my dad would be one of the most special memories of my life. It still is! I always feel a special connection with Dad (who passed away in 1997) as I go to midnight mass to sing in our church choir each Christmas Eve. Not a year goes by that I am not touched by the memory of that sacred night so many years ago.

COMING HOME
for Christmas

Cousins on Featherbeds

Donna Goodman
Sterlington, LA

Back in the late 1950s and early 1960s I grew up in a rural area south of Delhi, Louisiana, where my dad was a farmer. Christmas was a special time of sharing with all those wonderful cousins that my family didn't get to see very often. Every Christmas Eve day, my family carefully packed all of the presents (and other items that Santa might need) into the trunk of our car to head to PaPaw's house in Baskin, about 15 miles away. My parents were so good at this that my brothers and I had not a clue that Santa needed some help. At the same time, in other parts of the state, my cousins' parents were doing the same thing. Arrival at PaPaw's house was followed by a mad dash to claim the best (and warmest) bed. You see, the only heat in the house was a fireplace in the living room. Since all the kids had to sleep upstairs, it was a challenge to get either the room with the warm chimney running through it or the feather mattress. It was all in great fun, because with three cousins in the same bed, there wasn't much of a chance that we would get very cold! All the parents stayed up most of the night, so they were never ready to get up when the kids were. Of course, they always stalled, saying they had to get the fire built up to warm the house. Now, I know that it wasn't the fire that warmed the house, but the love of family sharing together in celebration of the birth of Christ.

Christmas Shoe Prizes

Ann Kiser-Ruth
Statesville, NC

I was born the ninth of 12 children in the Appalachian Mountains of Virginia. My mother was a homemaker and my dad worked in the coal mines. Most people would say we were poor, but now that I am grown, I truly know how rich we were in all things that are important. One of my fondest memories as a child was before Christmastime. We heated our house with wood and coal, and at night my dad would put all our little shoes around the stove. Some mornings we awoke to find a piece of candy or gum in them. Dad would tell us that Santa had left it, and that he was watching to make sure we were being good. I've continued this tradition with my own children and now with my precious granddaughter. Although my children are in their 20s, they still look for that first "shoe prize" on Thanksgiving morning.

Christmas Stockings

Deborah Parrish
Lubbock, TX

When I was young, every year we traveled from Texas to Georgia to celebrate Christmas with our grandparents. Since all our grandparents lived in the same small town, my parents had to come up with a creative way to share the festivities with both families. On Christmas Eve, we always attended midnight mass with my grandmother. When we returned home, Santa had left presents and we opened our gifts then. On Christmas morning, we visited our other grandparents, where Santa's elves had stuffed the stockings with small gifts, candy and fruit. My parents told us Santa had left these things behind for the elves to deliver. The stockings on Christmas morning are still treasured at our house and Christmas wouldn't be the same without them!

COMING HOME
for Christmas

Checking Santa's List

Sharon Wilson
Plumerville, AR

When I was four or five years old, I received a Little Golden Book of *Rudolph the Red-Nosed Reindeer*. My mom read it to me at bedtime, and I loved it. When we got to the page where Santa was using Rudolph's nose for a light to read the list of good boys and girls, though, my name was NOT on the list in the picture. I cried and cried because I knew I had been good! I think I cried myself to sleep. The next night my dad wanted to read me that story again, so I crawled up into his lap and miraculously my name was on the list! My sweet mom and dad had made sure that their little girl wasn't disappointed again. I still have that book.

Dad's Christmas Stories

Sherry Tysinger
Painesville, OH

I grew up in a rural area near the small town of Reedsville in southern Ohio. On Christmas Eve, my family always went to the Christmas Eve celebration at church. Then we'd come home, Dad would read us the Christmas story from our family Bible and we'd open one gift each. We were so excited! We never knew exactly what the story would be, but we always looked forward to it. On Christmas morning after opening presents, my husband David continues my dad's tradition, and always reads another Christmas story using his wonderful, preacher's speaking voice! Today he still reads a Christmas story to us all, including our grandchildren now. It wouldn't be Christmas to us without our "Dad's Christmas Stories!"

The Best Christmas Ever

Janis Parr
Ontario, Canada

My dad was a sergeant in the Royal Canadian Air Force and served for 27 years. In 1961, I was ten years old and halfway through the fifth grade when he was posted to Goose Bay, Labrador. While postings to different places were typical for us, this latest one was the hardest. We were a tightly knit family and we had never spent a Christmas apart from Dad. Because the house we were to move to wasn't ready, Dad went on ahead and we had to wait to join him. From the time he boarded the plane to fly to Goose Bay, I felt so sad, and as the weeks went by and Christmas drew nearer, I was just heartsick, missing him so much and knowing that possibly we might not even be together for Christmas. Then just two weeks before Christmas, we got the call! Mom, my brother Ron and I were transported to Goose Bay in an aircraft carrier...definitely not a luxury ride. I'll never forget seeing Dad standing on the airstrip, hardly recognizable in his heavy parka and fur hat, arms outstretched and the biggest smile on his face as we ran to him. I got there first! I ran into his arms and he spun me around and around. As cold as it was, we were warmed through and through to be together again. I will never forget the reunion we had, standing in the middle of the airfield in a blizzard. Being together again was the best Christmas present I could have ever asked for.

COMING HOME
for Christmas

My Christmas Memories

Cindy Long
Xenia, OH

When I was 12, my family moved to Norton, Ohio, three hours away from my grandparents, aunts, uncles and dozens of cousins. Before that, we were always at Grandma's for Christmas and that never changed. Mom would get the shopping done and the gifts wrapped, then Dad would load up the station wagon and off we'd go. Other family members from out of state also traveled to Grandma's home in Jamestown, Ohio, and of course all the aunts, uncles and cousins who lived nearby would come too after they had opened their gifts at home. In the evening, as everything quieted down, I would lie on my back with my head under Grandma and Grandpa's Christmas tree. It always smelled so good and the glass ornaments were so shiny, I could see my reflection in them. After relaxing there for awhile, I would run two doors down the street to my Aunt Carol and Uncle Bud's home. Then my aunt and I would begin wrapping gifts. For hours we stood at the dining room table and wrapped gifts. Uncle Bud would work on all the gifts that needed assembling. There were gifts for four children to get under the tree! The time I spent with Aunt Carol meant more to me that she will ever know. Then I would run back down the street to Grandma's, get ready for bed and crawl into one of her four-poster beds under so many quilts that I could hardly turn over. Morning would come quickly and everyone else began arriving. These were the best Christmases ever!

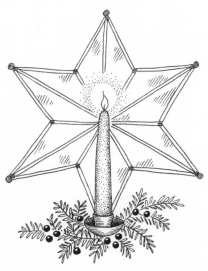

The Reason for the Season

Deeana Grasa
Riverview, FL

When our four girls Rebekah, Hannah, Hope and Eden were young, my husband and I started a tradition with them. Each night during December we would sit together as a family and share something that we'd done to make Jesus smile that day. This would have to be something done for someone else out of love. It was always so sweet to hear my little girls share what they had done. Then we would all put some raffia "hay" in a manger that I had made from grapevines. Each night we added more hay. On Christmas Eve, after the girls had gone to bed, I would lay a special Baby Jesus doll swaddled in simple cloth in the little manger. I will always remember our first year we did this. On that Christmas morning, the girls ran out to see if Baby Jesus was in the manger, not even looking for presents!

Today is Jesus' Birthday

Linda Schade
Troutman, NC

From the time I was an infant, I spent every Christmas Eve with my maternal grandparents here in Troutman, North Carolina. Santa always knew that I was there and never missed me! After I came downstairs to find my gifts from Santa, my parents and all of my mother's sisters and their husbands would arrive. After we ate breakfast, we would all go to the living room to open gifts. Before gifts were opened, we would sing a song, "Today Is Jesus' Birthday," that my mother had sung in church when she was five years old. Today, there are over 50 of us still getting together for Christmas, and we still sing that song before any gifts are opened!

Christmas in the Country

Barbara Feldner
Caldwell, OH

I am the eighth of nine children. The older children were 14 to 18 years older than we younger ones. I was born just as the war was ending in 1946, and times were hard. But on Christmas morning, the four younger kids would come flying down the stairs to see what Santa brought. We usually got pencils and a large yellow tablet with lines on it. I was so proud of mine and couldn't wait for school to start so I could use it. The older married kids brought us younger kids coloring books and crayons, and maybe a doll for me and guns and holsters for the boys. There were bowls of fresh oranges, hard candy and orange jelly slices for all to share too. The dinner my momma made was the best Christmas present of all. We all gathered around the table, said grace and enjoyed the family being together for the day. I would love to go back just one more time to a Christmas like that!

A Candlelit Breakfast

Gloria von Gesslein
Port Monmouth, NJ

My mom was an endless vessel of creative ideas for making wonderful memories. Like many families, we went through our hard times. One Christmas about ten years ago, money was especially tight. Food had to be stretched, and we couldn't even afford to put up a tree or give any gifts. We were pretty sad. However, we always kept on hand a big bag of tealights for emergencies when the lights went out during storms, as you could get a big bag of three dozen for three dollars. Early that Christmas morning, I woke up to a room softly glowing with tealights and the wonderful aroma of breakfast served in bed! Mom had made a little gift, wrapped it in aluminum foil and written down how she felt for me. That is one of the best memories I carry with me today.

A Christmas Tree Surprise

Wanda Rinella
Knoxville, TN

In Christmas of 1951, my parents, three brothers and I lived on a farm in rural Scottsburg, Indiana. There were no Christmas tree lots nearby, so we had to go out into the woods and choose our own. Our mother asked my brother Hurstan and me to go pick out that year's Christmas tree. We found a perfect tree filled with unusual pine cones and dragged it home through the snow. Mother set up the tree in our living room and we all decorated it together. It was so beautiful and we were so proud of it. The next morning when we woke up, we were amazed to see praying mantises flying all around the house! You see, what we thought were pine cones were actually cocoons and the heat from the house caused them to hatch! Needless to say, our parents did not let us pick out the family tree by ourselves after that. My kids have enjoyed this story every year and now the grandkids get a kick out of it too!

Socks from Aunt Noonie

Tammy Burnett
Springfield, MO

As a child growing up in Bellville, Ohio back in the 1970s, Christmas was such a magical time of year. All of our family would gather together to have a wonderful meal at Grandma's house, with the kids sitting in the kitchen, of course. Then the kids played games while the big folks talked and caught up on the year's events. When it came time to open gifts, my Great-Aunt Mildred (we lovingly called her Noonie) would give everyone her gift. It was always the same thing every year, a pair of socks, and they never fit! Not just the recipient, but you couldn't even trade because they didn't fit anyone at all! I love that memory and now we always try to have a gift of socks under the tree and a good laugh to follow.

COMING HOME
for Christmas

A Real Dog for Christmas

Jill Ross
Pickerington, OH

One year, when my sister was six and I was four, we were totally obsessed with dogs. We begged our parents to get us a dog, and spent all of our free time cutting pictures of dogs out of magazines. Our Christmas lists consisted of one item: a dog. A few weeks before Christmas, our neighbor came over to babysit us. We were just putting our finishing touches on our latest dog collages when our parents returned home, carrying a box. After admiring our artwork, my dad commented, "Why are we looking at pictures of dogs, when we have a real live dog right in this box?" In the box was a tiny brown puppy! He was a schnauzer and dachshund mix, and we named him Benji. It's one of my earliest and most treasured memories.

The Christmas Bicycle

Deborah Patterson
Carmichael, CA

I grew up in Citrus Heights, California. In 1963, my parents told me they didn't have the money for a bike that I so wanted. I taught myself to ride on a friend's bicycle for a few days by going downhill to get some speed up and getting my feet going long enough to pedal. Christmas came and there was no bike, so I was disappointed in Santa. Mom was making breakfast and asked if I would go get the bread out of the back of the truck. I thought that was a strange request, but I did it. Lo and behold, there was my bike, all shiny and new! I was never so excited in all my life! It was one of the best Christmases ever. Thanks, Mom and Dad!

Fireworks on Christmas Eve

Rebecca Ingle
Troutville, VA

When I was a child in the late 1950s, Christmas Eve was spent at my father's home place in Radford, Virginia, with my grandparents and numerous aunts, uncles, cousins, cousins and more cousins. We would gather in a house brimming with food, a cedar tree cut from nearby fields, dozens of gifts and music provided by family members adding to the excitement. After we had stuffed ourselves and each gift was opened, my cousins and I would wrap up and follow Granddaddy Beasley into the cold night air, through the yard and behind the barn where the most unusual Christmas celebration would begin. We would look towards the heavens and breathlessly wait for the biggest treat of the night...fireworks! Huge bursts of many colors exploded over our heads as we yelled into the night air, "Merry Christmas!" to each other. Many of those faces are gone now, but these events left a lasting impression on my life. Now, as every Christmas Eve night approaches, I go outside, look skyward and recall those precious moments and say, "Merry Christmas...I'll never forget!"

A Noisy New Year's Eve

Suzanne Bernier
Moses Lake, WA

My mom grew up here in Moses Lake, Washington and her grandpa had grown up in Ohio. When she was a little girl back in the early 1970s, on New Year's Eve she used to stand outside on the front porch with her mom and grandma holding an odd assortment of pots, pans and wooden spoons. When the clock struck midnight, they would bang on the pots and pans and make lots of noise while yelling out, "Happy New Year!" She handed this tradition down to my brother and me when we were little. Now that I'm grown up I've decided to carry on this tradition as well!

INDEX

Appetizers

Beverages

Breads

Breakfasts

INDEX

INDEX

Have a taste for more?

We created our official Circle of Friends so we could fill everyone in on the latest scoop at once. Visit us online to join in the fun and discover free recipes, exclusive giveaways and much more!

www.gooseberrypatch.com

Call us toll-free at 1·800·854·6673

U.S. to Metric Recipe Equivalents

Volume Measurements

1/4 teaspoon	1 mL
1/2 teaspoon	2 mL
1 teaspoon	5 mL
1 tablespoon = 3 teaspoons	15 mL
2 tablespoons = 1 fluid ounce	30 mL
1/4 cup	60 mL
1/3 cup	75 mL
1/2 cup = 4 fluid ounces	125 mL
1 cup = 8 fluid ounces	250 mL
2 cups = 1 pint =16 fluid ounces	500 mL
4 cups = 1 quart	1 L

Weights

1 ounce	30 g
4 ounces	120 g
8 ounces	225 g
16 ounces = 1 pound	450 g

Oven Temperatures

300° F	150° C
325° F	160° C
350° F	180° C
375° F	190° C
400° F	200° C
450° F	230° C

Baking Pan Sizes

Square

8x8x2 inches	2 L = 20x20x5 cm
9x9x2 inches	2.5 L = 23x23x5 cm

Rectangular

13x9x2 inches	3.5 L = 33x23x5 cm

Loaf

9x5x3 inches	2 L = 23x13x7 cm

Round

8x1-1/2 inches	1.2 L = 20x4 cm
9x1-1/2 inches	1.5 L = 23x4 cm